THE BOOK WE TEACH

J. B. Weatherspoon, M.A., Th.D., D.D.

NASHVILLE, TENNESSEE
THE SUNDAY SCHOOL BOARD
of the
SOUTHERN BAPTIST CONVENTION

Printed in the United States of America
10,000—4-35—3

CONTENTS

FOREWORD

This book is written and offered primarily for use in the Training Course for Sunday School Workers provided by the Sunday School Board of the Southern Baptist Convention. We seek to offer in this Course carefully-prepared handbooks which will guide and stimulate workers in the Sunday school.

The Course, together with the conditions proposed for its study, is provided for a widely-varying constituency. The books may be offered as texts in colleges and seminaries; they will be studied most largely by busy workers whose minds are occupied with the cares of life. In the effort to meet these varied needs, optional books are offered throughout. In general, no specific books in the Course are required for any award, alternate books and choices being everywhere provided.

The helps and directions for study are proposed primarily for busy workers. When the books are offered in educational institutions and under other conditions which justify and demand higher standards, such higher standards will of course be observed.

Directions for the Study of this Book

I. *When the Work is Done in Class*

1. At least ten class periods, forty-five minutes in the clear, shall be offered

2. Those desiring awards shall—

   (1) Attend at least seven class periods

   (2) Take a written examination making a minimum grade of seventy per cent, and

   (3) Certify that they have carefully read the textbook.

When it seems impracticable to meet these requirements class members will do the writing required of individual students and send in their manuscripts.

The class teacher, on accepting assignment to teach the class, should send for report blanks. These blanks must be filled out, and the above requirements must be fully met before awards can be granted.

The books should be read during class-study. In case this seems impracticable, a pledge to read the book within the next two weeks will be accepted.

II. *When the Work is Done Individually or by Correspondence*

No examination will be required. Students will make choice of the following:

1. Write answers to the questions printed in the book, or

2. Write a development or elaboration of the chapter outlines.

Correspondence students will study the book in their own way. Then with the open book and any other helps available they will write answers to the printed questions, or they will, if they prefer, write a development or elaboration of the chapter outlines. In either case the students will find it necessary to study the book carefully, to rethink its message and state in their own language its essential teachings.

All written work done by such students will be sent to the Educational Department of the Baptist Sunday School Board, Nashville, Tennessee.

P. E. Burroughs,
Educational Secretary.

CHAPTER ONE

A LIBRARY OF SACRED LITERATURE

The term "Bible" according to its original derivation means "the books." In the fourth century Jerome spoke of the Bible as the "Divine Library." Although we possess it in one volume, there are sixty-six "books," varying in length from a brief personal letter to great volumes, comprising a great library of sacred writings. It cannot be read in a day; it cannot be fully known in a lifetime.

In a real sense, however, the sixty-six books are one book. Like a mosaic, or a piece of tapestry, or an organism such as the human body, its varieties compose a beautiful unity. Every part fits in, adding its contribution of truth and light. Among Christians it is *the Book of Books* and it is the greatest book in the world. More than any other it belongs to the whole world. Its teachings concern all nations and races. Its ministry is world-wide. Translated into more languages and dialects than any other (about 800), and not approached by any other in the volume of its distribution, it is speaking constantly to a public comprising many millions. Unlike other books that are best sellers for a year, its favor lives and increases from generation to generation. Put into the hands of a child learning to read it remains a precious possession unto old age, furnishing life and inspiration and hope across the years.

This Divine Library, this Book of Books is the Sunday school teacher's textbook. And it is for him that the chapters of this book are written. In order to create in his pupils a living interest, to guide them into a true acceptance and understanding, and to bring them into a living fellowship with our God and Saviour, the teacher must make good and effective use of his Bible. To him it must be increasingly interesting, intelligible, and imperative. It is in order to help at these points that our study is made.

We begin with an examination of the Bible in its external aspects. What is the Bible as we have it? How are its books arranged and classified? How did it come into existence? How did it come to be accepted as the Holy Scriptures of our religion? How was it transmitted to us across the centuries and in our language?

I. The Bible As We Have It

In broadest outline the Bible has two great divisions: The Old Testament, which is composed of thirty-nine books (Genesis to Malachi); the New Testament, which has twenty-seven books (Matthew to Revelation). The word "testament" means in this usage "covenant."

1. The Old Testament

(1) Jewish Division: The Old Testament was subdivided and classified by the Jews as follows: (1) *The Law* (Genesis, Exodus, Leviticus, Numbers, Deuteronomy). (2) *The Prophets,* which were in turn classified as (a) *Former* Prophets (Joshua, Judges, 1 and 2 Samuel, 1 and 2 Kings), and (b) *Latter* Prophets (Isaiah, Jeremiah, Ezekiel, the twelve minor prophets). (3) *The Writings,* as follows: (a) the poetical books (Psalms, Proverbs, Job); (b) the five rolls (Song of Solomon, Ruth, Lamentations, Ecclesiastes, Esther); (c) Daniel, Ezra, Nehemiah, and Chronicles.

(2) Modern Analysis: In modern times we do not feel the necessity of following the Jewish analysis very strictly, and are more familiar with the following classification: (1) *The Pentateuch* (= five books), or Hexateuch (adding Joshua to the first five books). (2) The *Historical Books* (Joshua, Judges, Ruth, 1 and 2 Sam-

uel, 1 and 2 Kings, 1 and 2 Chronicles, Ezra, Nehemiah, and Esther). (3) The *Poetical and Wisdom Books* (Job, Psalms, Proverbs, Ecclesiastes, Song of Solomon, and Lamentations). (4) The *Prophetical Books,* subdivided into the *major* prophets (Isaiah, Jeremiah, Ezekiel, and Daniel) and the *minor* prophets (the twelve shorter books of prophecy). This grouping follows the order of books found in our Bibles, rather than the order of their composition which is very difficult to determine.

2. The New Testament

The New Testament yields naturally the following divisions: (1) *The Four Gospels* (Matthew, Mark, Luke, John). They do not give a complete biography of Jesus, but they do give a glorious presentation of his Humanity, his Messiahship, his compassionate Saviourhood, and his Deity. (2) *The Acts of the Apostles,* which records the progress of the Christian faith in the Roman Empire from the Ascension of Christ to the closing years of Paul's ministry. (3) *The Epistles of Paul* (thirteen in number), which may be divided into two groups: (a) those written *to churches* (Romans, 1 and 2 Corinthians, Galatians, Ephesians, Philippians, Colossians, 1 and 2 Thessalonians); and (b) those written *to individuals* (1 and 2 Timothy, Titus, Philemon). (4) *The General or Catholic Epistles* (Hebrews, James, 1 and 2 Peter, 1, 2, and 3 John, Jude), so called because for the most part "the wider interests of the churches at large are prominent rather than the problem of one particular church." 2 and 3 John, however, are personal rather than general. (5) *The Book of Revelation,* which in vision and symbol encourages the persecuted Christian communities to patience and hope, as it pictures the conflicts and final triumph of Christ and the kingdom of God.

II. How the Old Testament Came To Be

Volumes have been written concerning the origin of the Old Testament and there is no general agreement on all particulars. But we may set down some of the results of the investigations of devout scholars which will give us an intelligent view of how the Law, the Prophets, and the Writings came to be.

1. *The Law,* called also the five books of Moses, contains the story of the creation of the world, the early experiences of the race, the history of the Hebrew people from the call of Abram to the end of the life of Moses. It also includes the great body of laws which through their history served to guide the Israelites.

On the basis of the various statements in these books that Moses wrote and was commanded of God to write, *tradition has held through the centuries that Moses was their author.* If there was a man capable of writing, who wanted to give to a nation the abiding inspiration and faith and guidance most needed in its formative years, nothing could have been more suitable than to write just these books at that period in Israel's life. And Moses was such a man. He was a learned man, filled with a sense of the divine mission of his people, and committed wholly to their life and blessing. Nothing was more natural than that he should write down not only the laws received in the mount, but also the background and ideals that were to be the nation's inspiration; nothing more to be expected than that God should have put it into his heart so to do.

2. *The Prophets and Writings* cover a long period from Joshua's day to some time after the return from captivity.

(1) What was said above about the use of materials applies in a large way to the *historical books.* Every period had its chroniclers. Joshua, the successor of Moses, was a writer (Joshua 8:30ff; 24:26). Even in the dark and critical period of the Judges the heroes did not lack for faithful chroniclers. Particularly from the period of David there were many writers. Besides the court scribes (copyists) and chroniclers there were

the prophets. The writers of Kings and Chronicles refer to at least ten other books, including the writings of or about Solomon, Samuel, Nathan, Gad, Iddo, and Jehu. In such writings as these, growing in volume with the years, much material was at hand when men were moved to their sacred task. And with the great historical books before us it is easy to conclude that *at the close of each great epoch some prophet or prophets took up the task of bringing together the great events of the period,* producing, for example, "Joshua" after the conquest of Canaan; "Judges," after the kingdom was established; "Samuel," after the death of the great David; "Kings," after the nation had gone into captivity; and "Chronicles" (perhaps by a priest or priests), after the decree of Restoration and the renewal of worship in the homeland.

(2) While this was going on the *prophetical books* were also being written. We are to think of them in general as the writings of the men whose names they bear. Whether all the prophets left the books just as we have them, or whether they were sometimes assembled by faithful scribes is of secondary consideration. For example, two of Dr. A. B. Davidson's greatest books were assembled from his lectures by others after his death. Happily we have Jeremiah's own account of how his book was written. After he had been preaching over twenty years God commanded him to write down all his messages in a book (Jer. 36). This he did with the help of Baruch, his scribe. When this book was destroyed by the king at least a year later, it was rewritten in the same way. At this second writing many other words were added—presumably the prophecies of the intervening year. In like manner Baruch would continue to record in the book the prophet's further utterances, and to preserve them as God's message to his people through the prophet. In some such way we may think of the Books of Isaiah, Ezekiel, and the others.

(3) A study of the *poetical and wisdom books* discloses in Psalms and Proverbs still another method of composition—they are collections of collections. There are five books in our Book of Psalms (see American Revised Version). These collections were made at different periods, from David's day until after the Exile, for purposes of worship. The Psalms are of all ages, one of them being ascribed to Moses, many of them to David, others to Solomon, Asaph, sons of Korah, and so forth, on to the post-exilic period when all were brought together in one great psalter. Likewise, Proverbs is composed of several collections of the proverbs of Solomon and others, dating from Solomon himself, who was famous for his wisdom, down at least to Hezekiah's day 250 years later (Prov. 25: 1).

3. *When and how did these writings become for the Hebrews their Bible,* a part of the canon (i. e., the accepted list of sacred writings from whose class other writings were excluded)? This question cannot be answered exactly. We may confidently say that the canon "began with the first laying up of the 'book of the law' before Jehovah" (Deut. 31:25f). Throughout the nation's life, from Moses on, "the Law" was held sacred. But what about the Prophets and Writings? We must remember that large editions could not be issued from a printing press as in modern times, but all writing had to be copied by hand. Accordingly, the books of prophecy and history, the collections of psalms and proverbs would not be at once the possession of the whole nation. *These books had to become known and had to prove themselves to have been written by true prophets and inspired by God.* We may believe, however, that from their first appearance they had the value of Holy Scripture "to the godly who knew and used them." Thus their acceptance and separation from other writings was gradual. And the tradition may be held as true that, after the sifting period of the Exile, in the age of Ezra and Nehemiah, the body of

Sacred Scriptures in its three parts became in the main a fixed library. It was not done arbitrarily, nor by a single act or decision of any council. The spirit of God was in the recognition as in the composition of these great books. That a few of them were questioned later by some and that other books were included by some, or that additions to the "Writings" were accepted after Ezra's day, does not mean that the nation did not have its Bible. It was not date, but a conviction of their inspiration that gained acceptance for them, and gave to the Jews their Bible which is also a part of our Bible.

III. How the New Testament Came To Be

Under what circumstances were the books of the New Testament written? And how did they come to be accepted as Holy Scriptures?

1. *The circumstances* which were used of God to call the New Testament writers to their task are fairly discernible.

(1) *At first,* after Christ's ascension, the Apostles seem to have had no intention of writing. They had their Bible—the Old Testament—and to add to it was as foreign to their thoughts as additions to our Bible are from ours. Christ had not written. Nor had he commanded them to write. Their business was to bear witness to him, to make and baptize disciples, to teach them his teachings. And this they did, with the result that soon there were thousands of believers in Palestine and distant lands, Jews and Gentiles. Only a few had been the companions of Jesus, but all wanted his words and the full story of his wonderful works. They wanted the record for their own satisfaction, and they needed it for witnessing. His miracles, parables, discourses, unfoldings of the Scriptures, the Apostles' experience of him, and their interpretation of his words and works—all these must not perish with the passing of

the aging eye-witnesses. Nor was it the purpose of God that they should pass.

(2) *Accordingly certain men were led to record the "Gospels"* as we have them. Mark was first, a vivid portrayal of the active ministry and divine power of Christ. Next was Matthew, written with the Jewish people especially in mind, showing that Jesus is the fulfillment of the Old Testament messianic hope. Then came Luke, written by the first Christian historian who wrote also the Acts. Luke says in his introduction (1: 1-4, ASV) that many others had "taken in hand to draw up a narrative concerning those matters which have been fulfilled among us," and that his purpose was to give an accurate and orderly account of them. There must be no confusion as to facts among the witnesses of the Saviour. This passion for an accurate and true witness is present in every part of the New Testament.

(3) These three Gospels not only illustrate how the work of witnessing called for the written word, but the further fact that *all the books of the New Testament are the answers to certain situations.* For instance, after a few years of missionary work there were Christian churches in various Gentile communities. They met many problems and dangers both within and without their own fellowship. It was to meet these difficulties that such letters as James and the Thessalonian and Corinthian letters of Paul were written. Again there were theological problems as in Galatia, Rome, and Ephesus, or conflicts with certain active heresies which called forth the Gospel of John, the Epistles to the Hebrews, Colossians, and others. Persecution also appears as the particular circumstance behind Jude, the Epistles of Peter, and Revelation.

(For those who desire to study these backgrounds of the New Testament writings the excellent book of Dr. W. O. Carver, *How the New Testament Came to Be Written,* is recommended.)

2. *The Method of composition* of the New Testament books differs little from that of the Old Testament. The writers drew upon all the ordinary sources of knowledge. Both tradition and evidence from his book itself indicate that *Mark* received much of his material from Peter, who spoke at first hand. *Luke* says plainly that he "traced the course of all things accurately from the first." As Paul's companion he came into contact with many Christians, including the Apostles and other early Christians who had lived in the time of Jesus. In addition he had also the writings of others (1:1), including Mark's Gospel.

The writers of the Epistle to the *Hebrews* and of *Matthew* drew upon the Old Testament. Paul drew upon his rich knowledge of the Old Testament in its theological, legal, ceremonial, and ethical teachings, as also upon his accurate knowledge of the world of his day. Both he and *John* display an accurate understanding of the pagan philosophies of the time. And John in Revelation adopts the literary method of the apocalyptic writers of the time. That is to say, the New Testament writers were students, and employed the methods of students in their work. This fact does not exclude the ideas of inspiration and revelation, but rather indicates the method of the Divine Spirit in revealing and recording for humanity the Word of God.

3. *How did these writings become a part of the Christian's Bible?* As in the case of the Old Testament it was not by a definite and authoritative decision of some council, but gradually as the conviction of their apostolic origin and divine inspiration grew. By the time the last of them (Revelation) was written (about 95 A.D.) the Gospels were being read in the services of worship along with the prophets, and the Epistles of Paul were being copied and circulated widely among the churches. It took considerable time for some of the books to be widely circulated, as for instance the purely

personal letter, Philemon; and others were naturally delayed if their apostolic origin or their doctrines were questioned. The gradual but constant pressure of the books upon the attention of the churches, with a steadily widening recognition may be easily traced in early church history. By the end of the second century the term "New Testament" was already in use. In 331 A.D. Eusebius listed as Christian Scriptures all the books of our New Testament and no others. In 365 A.D. Athanasius gave a list of the New Testament books which is identical with our New Testament. So step by step the New Testament came to universal recognition, and we may say with Patterson Smyth, "If anything is clearly taught by this story, it is this—that the Canon of Scripture was formed not suddenly by some startling miracle, not officially by some decision of Synod, or Bishop, or prophet or saint, but slowly, gradually, half consciously, by the quiet influence of the Holy Spirit in the minds of the men of the Church."

IV. How the Bible Was Transmitted to Us

1. The first translation of the Scriptures was that of the Old Testament into Greek, which was made in Egypt in the third and second centuries (about 200 B.C.) for the Jews and Jewish proselytes who were unable to read the Hebrew. As Greek became increasingly the common world language this version, called the Septuagint (LXX) attained a wider circulation, and was in common use even in Palestine in the time of Jesus. Many of the quotations in the New Testament are from the Septuagint.

2. The first important step in the direction of the English Bible was the work of Jerome at the end of the fourth century A.D. (390-405). He translated the entire Bible into Latin. His version came to be called the Vulgate, after the sixth century, because it had attained general use in the Roman Catholic Church.

3. In the fourteenth century *John Wyclif* translated the Bible into English. The appearance of his work aroused great opposition, but it was widely circulated, and its influence had much to do in preparing the English people for the Reformation. His translation was from the Latin Vulgate, a translation of a translation.

4. The next English translation of note was that of the New Testament by *Tyndale* in the sixteenth century, for which he suffered martyrdom in 1536. An important fact is that he used the New Testament Greek text of Erasmus. Since Wyclif's day the printing press had been invented, and now books could be issued rapidly and at smaller cost. It was accordingly impossible to suppress the Bible's circulation. The church had to give it an open door, and by the end of the century five other English translations had appeared.

5. Then came the *King James Version* (1611), a translation authorized by the King and made by the best scholars of the time. By its excellence and royal authorization it stopped the fever of translation that had followed Tyndale's work; and today, after 300 years, it is the most used English version.

6. By the closing years of the nineteenth century there was among scholars of England and America a feeling that there ought to be a new translation. This was in the light of such facts as the following: (a) Meanings of many words had changed within the three centuries. (b) There were available many ancient manuscripts in Hebrew and Greek, various old versions, and writings of Christian fathers which were not known in 1611, which would yield a more correct text. (c) There was need of paragraphing and distinctive printing of poetical portions which were not observed in the old version. Accordingly, a Revision Committee was organized which produced the Revised Version (1881-1885). The American members of that committee, not satisfied with the work, produced in 1901-1904 the

American Revised Version, which is in wide use today. Since that time there have also appeared a number of translations by individual scholars, particularly of the New Testament. Although others are superior to the King James Version in accuracy and understandableness, it is still in the ascendency, and it will probably be long before it will be superseded in popular usage.

Thus the Divine Library has been written, preserved, and transmitted to us. It cost the diligent and courageous toil of men at every step of the way, often persecution and suffering, sometimes death. But by the grace and providence of God we have it. It was his will to reveal it in human experience, to form it by human toil, to preserve it by human loyalty. And it is in our hands, God's Word to the world, that we may learn its heavenly message and pass it on to those whom God has committed to our charge.

REVIEW QUESTIONS

1. In what sense is the Bible a library? In what sense a book?

2. Give the Jewish classification of the books of the Old Testament.

3. What classification is generally made by Christians?

4. Give a general classification of the New Testament books.

5. Who was the responsible author of the Pentateuch? What bearing do the use of existing material and the later addition of laws have upon his authorship?

6. How did the historical books of the Old Testament come to be written?

7. Tell about the writing of Jeremiah and the Psalms.

8. How did these books come to be the Hebrew Bible?

9. Describe in general the circumstances which led to the writing of the Gospels and Epistles of the New Testament.

10. How did Luke go about his writing?

11. How and when did these New Testament writings become a part of the Christian's Bible?

12. Who was the first translator of the Bible into English? Explain the production of the King James Version and the American Revised Version.

FOR THE BLACKBOARD

A Library of Sacred Literature

A Divine Library. The Book of Books.
The Sunday School Teacher's Textbook

I. The Bible as We Have It
   1. The Old Testament. Jewish division. Modern analysis
   2. The New Testament. Analysis

II. How the Old Testament Came to Be
   1. The Law. Mosaic authorship. Two questions concerning authorship
   2. The Prophets and Writings
      (1) The writing of the historical books
      (2) How the prophetical books were written
      (3) The composition and collection of the poetical and wisdom books
   3. When and how did these writings become sacred Scriptures?

III. How the New Testament Came to Be
   1. The circumstances calling for Christian literature
      (1) At the first
      (2) The need for the gospels
      (3) How the other books came to be written
   2. The method of composition. Examples
   3. How the New Testament books became a part of the Christian Bible

IV. How the Bible Was Transmitted to Us
   1. The first translation of the Scriptures
   2. The work of Jerome
   3. Wyclif's Bible
   4. Tyndale's translation of the New Testament, introducing a period of translation
   5. The King James Version
   6. The Revised Version. Why needed. The American Revised Version

CHAPTER TWO

A BOOK OF RELIGION AND REVELATION

Having studied in Chapter One some of the more external facts connected with the contents, composition, and preservation of the Bible, we must now ask about its nature. With what is the Bible concerned? What kind of book is it? For what purpose was it written? And of what value is it for us today?

I. A Book of Religion

1. *Evident everywhere* is this fact—that the Bible is a book of religion. The center and circumference of its interest is religion, the relationship between God and man, and the meaning of that relationship for life here and hereafter. Its subject matter includes the natural world of things; the human struggle with social and economic problems, moral and intellectual problems; but its purpose is not scientific, or sociological, or historical, but religious—that men may know God and his will, and be brought into fellowship with him.

2. This fact *explains the Bible's treatment of history* and human events in general. It explains why things that seem of greatest importance to the secular or scientific mind are passed over with few words, while much space is given to the matters that are of interest only to the spiritually alert. We may take an illustration from the Old Testament. In Genesis the long ages from creation down to about 2000 B.C. are compassed in less than ten pages. The whole period of creation's six incalculable "days" is covered in a single chapter. But in the same book more than twelve pages are given to the story of Abraham, and fourteen pages to the life of Joseph. If the purpose of the book had been scientific or historical, these facts would be beyond explana-

tion. But why was Genesis written? Was it not to show that the very life of the Hebrew nation was rooted in God, the Creator and Ruler of the world? Not creation, but the Creator and his relation to Abraham, Jacob, and Joseph, to the past, present, and future of Israel in things great and small, were at the center. Once this religious purpose of the book and the introductory character of the first eleven chapters are seen, the proportions are understood. Other illustrations of this truth will be noticed in Chapter Three.

3. That the Bible is a book of religion is also *a key to some of its silences.* Let us turn to the New Testament for an illustration of this. The New Testament does not directly condemn autocracy, or the evil institution of slavery, or war. Why these silences? The answer is that they are not the silences of unconcern, but the silences of a purpose that was deeper than temporary or local reform. Jesus saw life to the bottom. He did not see it as a set of separate compartments—economic, political, religious, public, private—to each of which he must fit a peculiar code of morals. He saw all human relationships as subject to one body of principles, and these the fruit and expression of religion in the heart. And the New Testament, which was written in the spirit of Jesus, had the same religious point of view. It did not attack slavery directly; it went deeper and taught the inestimable value and the dignity of personality in the sight of God. It did not declaim against war, but it taught a love for humanity that will finally outlaw it on principle rather than command. It did not outline a new economic order, but it exposed the dangers of wealth, the evils of exploitation and covetousness. That is to say, it laid the ax at the root of these evils in the human spirit and offered a religion that would change life from the center.

4. Let it be noted also that the Bible is *a book of one religion.* From first to last there is the same re-

ligion. To be sure there was growth in its teachings, a progressive understanding of the essentials of that religion as we shall notice presently, but there are not two or three religions. It proclaims the same God from Genesis to Revelation. Abraham did not know as much about God as John did, but their God was the same. There was much idolatry in Israel all along until the Exile, but it was always denounced as an evil. There was no writer of the Scriptures who was not a monotheist. And the one God of the Bible is a God of grace with a redemptive purpose, which finds expression in a thousand ways as the story unfolds from Genesis to Revelation. Questions, doubts, sins are faithfully recorded; the religion of many spoken of in the Bible was fickle and changing; but the religion which is preached and contended for by the Bible is one religion, and that religion is its central concern.

II. A Book of Revelation

That the Bible is a book of religion in its central subject matter, point of view, and purpose, prepares us for its claim to be also a book of revelation. For essentially religion has two sides,—man's outreach toward God and God's revelation of himself to man. Only reality in the latter as well as sincerity in the former makes religion true and authentic. And the belief of Christians is that the religion of the Bible is a revealed religion and that the Bible itself is an inspired record of that revelation.

The process of this revelation is to be seen in the experiences of individual men and nations, especially the nation of Israel. We have already seen in Chapter One some of the steps in the making of the Bible. Men wrote out of their experiences and to meet certain circumstances; they engaged in research; they selected some materials and rejected others; out of a wealth of Hebrew and Christian literature they gathered our

Bible. The human factor is prominent. But as we study the Bible we cannot escape the conviction that there was everywhere the Divine accompaniment, the urge and guidance of the Divine Spirit in research, in selection, in interpretation, in song and prophecy, and in the resultant record. And this not because we come to the Bible with any pre-formed theory of what we ought to find, but *because of what we actually find there.* The question to be answered by the teacher then is: What do we find in the Bible that would lead us to accept it as from God?

1. We find first that *in many places in the Bible the writers claim the authority of God for their words.* Many, many times in the Pentateuch it is said, "Jehovah spoke unto Moses, saying . . ." He is said to have spoken to Samuel and other prophets who are named, between the time of Moses and that of the writing prophets. That God revealed himself to his people was in the faith of the Hebrews from earliest times. When we come to the writing prophets every one of them without exception claims to be an instrument of Divine revelation. Such expressions as the following appear many times, ASV: "The word of Jehovah that came to Joel"; "Thus saith Jehovah"; "The vision of Isaiah which he saw"; "The word of Jehovah came unto me, saying." Such is the Old Testament claim.

Turning to the New Testament we find everywhere an acceptance of the Old Testament as the word of God. Paul speaks of it in these words: "Every scripture inspired of God" (2 Tim. 3: 16, ASV); and Peter says, "No prophecy ever came by the will of man: but men spake from God, being moved by the Holy Spirit" (2 Peter 1: 21, ASV). In Hebrews 1: 1, ASV, we read: "God having of old time spoken unto the fathers in the prophets." And above all, the testimony of Jesus is to the same effect. All his references to the Scriptures (*i. e.,* the Old Testament) take their divine origin for granted. Compare Matt. 4; Matt. 22: 29, 43; John 5: 39. "With Jesus it was a commonplace thought that the Old Testament was God's self-revelation," is Doctor Mullins' expression. And Kirkpatrick writes: "From the whole treatment of the Old Testament Scriptures in the New Testament, even more than from explicit statement, it is clear that they are regarded as being of Divine origin."

But what about the New Testament? For his words and works Jesus claimed the authority of his Father, and the Gospels, faithful to the facts, record God's self-revelation in the person, words, and works of Christ. Moreover, although Jesus did not as far as we know command the Apostles to write, he promised them the Holy Spirit (John 14 and 15) who would guide them in their knowledge of the truth and in their witness. When one reads 1 Corinthians 2:10-13; 14: 37; 1 Thess. 4: 2; Gal. 1: 12; 2: 2, he cannot doubt Paul's claim to the guidance of the Holy Spirit in his interpretation of the gospel, although he does not claim in his letters the "Thus saith the Lord" of the prophets. It is very significant also, as showing the estimate others put upon Paul's writings, that Peter should write: "Even as our beloved brother Paul also, *according to the wisdom given to him, wrote* unto you; as also in *all* his epistles, speaking in them of these things; wherein are some things hard to be understood, which the ignorant and unstedfast wrest, *as they do also the other scriptures,* unto their own destruction" (2 Peter 3: 15, 16, ASV).

2. A second thing we find in the Bible that points to its divine source is *the nature of its great themes and the character of its teachings.* On this point Dr. E. C. Dargan wrote: "It bears upon itself, in the truths which it reveals, in the exalted moral character of its teachings, in the permanency and power of its influence, the proofs of its divine authorship. No other book in all literature has borne, or bears, such a char-

acter as this." Among its grand themes are *God* in his unity and holiness, and in his creative and redemptive work; *man* in his original nature, his sin and redemption; the *kingdom of God* as pre-visioned and foretold in messianic prophecy, and as fulfilled in and through *Jesus Christ, the Son of God,* and administered by the *Holy Spirit* in the hearts of men; *divine atonement;* and *immortality.* Such high doctrines were not discovered except as they were revealed. Their content is not the fruit of unaided human thought, but of communication between the Spirit of God and the spirit of man. In its answer to the deep longings and problems of humanity the Bible introduces ideas, and rises to heights of moral and spiritual vision, to which no other literature has ever reached. Its writers saw God revealing himself in the history of the chosen nation; they divined his purpose to establish a kingdom in righteousness; they saw the spiritual and moral demands of this order upon men; they saw Jesus Christ as God's supreme revelation of himself; they experienced in themselves his presence and his voice. And each in his own day wrote the vision and burden of his soul, as he was moved by the Holy Spirit. That God was speaking through his chosen prophets and Apostles is the only adequate explanation of this amazing book.

III. A Book of Growing Light

1. To the fact that the Bible is a book of religion which is a divine revelation must be added another, namely, that *God revealed himself and his truth gradually.* To some this may be a new thought—that the revelation recorded in the Bible has not the same completeness and light in Abraham's day as in that of Moses, in Moses' day as in Jeremiah's, in Jeremiah's day as in the New Testament. Once it is realized, however, the Bible becomes a richer and more understandable book. Revelation began in the childhood of the race, and continued through its expanding expe-

rience, shining, like the rising sun, with increasing brightness until the noonday light appeared in the person, word, and work of Jesus Christ. The Epistle to the Hebrews notes this fact in its opening verses: "God having of old time spoken unto the fathers in the prophets *by divers portions* and *in divers manners*, hath at the end of these days spoken unto us in his Son," ASV. In portions and ways that the succeeding ages could apprehend he disclosed himself and his will for humanity. And how could it have been otherwise? It was in every age as Jesus found in the case of his disciples: "I have yet many things to say unto you, but ye cannot bear them now" (John 16: 12, ASV). God's purpose and his willingness to reveal himself were the same from the first, but he was limited by human dulness and blindness and incapacity. And the Bible, faithful to the course of the revelation, records the progress of the growing light.

2. *Two illustrations* of the fact will be enough to indicate how the great ideas of the Bible grew and expanded from less to more.

(1) We give one example in the illuminating words of Doctor Mullins: "The *conception of Jehovah* himself is first presented with emphasis on the attribute of power. He is thought of chiefly in his relation with Israel. Slowly the idea is transformed into the splendid conception of Isaiah in which Jehovah is portrayed as infinite in all his attributes, and yet full of condescension, grace, and love. In the New Testament we have the crowning revelation of God as the infinite Father who sends his Son to redeem the world."

(2) The same is true of the *idea of righteousness*. There was a day when men said "an eye for an eye" was right. Retaliation and blood revenge, hatred of enemies and cruel slaughter were at one with the standard of righteousness. But God's light grew, and step by step the ideas advanced to a law of love and forgiveness. David's prayer for the cursing and de-

struction of his foes gave way to the prayers of Jesus and Stephen for the forgiveness of their enemies, as the right attitude, the expression of the divine counsel. See also the contrasts in Matt. 5: 21-48. Doctor Mullins' conclusion here also is worthy of quotation: "There is growth from immature forms of morality in the early parts of the Old Testament to a perfected morality in the New Testament which presents a striking contrast between the outward and inward, the temporary and permanent, the special and the universal, the provisional and the final."

3. What is *the significance of the progressiveness of revelation* to Christian teachers and all Christians?

(1) Certainly it means that we *must not study the Bible piecemeal.* It has been truly said that "the truth of Bible revelation is reserved for him who searches for it not in a part of the Scriptures but through their whole range." Much in the Old Testament is provisional, temporary, and incomplete; there is growth there, "but it is like the plant developing from stalk to bud, and from bud to flower, there is a final stage yet to come—that of the ripened fruit," which is found in the New Testament. So we are not to use as final and complete just any statement except as it is interpreted in the light of the total message of the Bible. Many false teachings have boasted biblical support by disregarding its progressive revelation and its unity.

(2) To think of revelation as a growing light *explains many moral difficulties in the Old Testament.* God spoke to men in the light of their experience; his commands and teachings included not his absolute will, but his will for them at their stage of religious and ethical progress. For example, (a) the Law of Moses recognized polygamy (Deut. 21:15), and made easy provision for divorce, concerning which Jesus gave an enlightening explanation: "Moses for your hardness of heart suffered you to put away your wives." Polyg-

amy and divorce found a place in the economy of God for Israel, not because they expressed a perfect morality, but because Israel could not see and accept anything higher. But it is to be observed that through legal and prophetic restraints he kept lifting them toward permanent monogamy. (b) Another example is the religious sanction of war in the Old Testament. The principle of progressive revelation assists us here by reminding us that in an age when violence was unbounded, and human life was cheap, an utter prohibition of violence and war would have seemed itself unethical. God was dealing with people who could not believe that war was wrong; but they could be led to fight not in hatred of men, or love of destruction, but against evil men and for constructive purposes. His love was such that he would speak a word that would lift, even though it did not lift them to perfection at one stroke. His ideal of love, peace and brotherhood was fully revealed in Christ, and one day war must go the way of individual murder and polygamy in Christendom.

The unideal commands of the Old Testament do not therefore involve God in moral failure, but proclaim a love that is patient and will not let go. This divine principle of action is illustrated in Christ's dealing with his disciples. At one stage he said to them "Go only to the lost sheep of the house of Israel" while even then his heart was burning to say what he later did say, "Go ye into all the world." He was not participating in Israel's sinful prejudices but dealing with his disciples and commanding them on the basis of their capacity and their understanding.

(3) *The question of the Bible and Science is also relieved.* The Old Testament used the language of its own age, which was the language of appearance in describing natural phenomena. The "science" of the Old Testament no more precludes progress in scientific knowledge than its ethics precludes ethical ad-

vance. The wonder is not the technical disharmony between the Bible and science, but the real harmony that enlightened interpretation on both sides is finding.

IV. A Book of Sure Guidance

The Bible speaks a sure word. It is not the record of a human search that ends in uncertainty. Its final word is always positive even in such books as Job and Ecclesiastes. Without any note of uncertainty the Bible proclaims its gospel of God, our Creator and Redeemer. Need we have any doubt concerning that of which it is so sure? Is it a book of sure guidance?

1. An affirmative answer *follows upon the nature of the Bible* as already set forth. If it is a record of God's revelation of himself, given to the world through men chosen and inspired for their task, and preserved through the centuries by his providence, then it follows that its light is true, and men who follow its teaching find God.

Only those who go to the Bible seeking what it was not given to supply, or with insincerity of spirit, are disappointed. We must remember that it is a book of religion. It does not invite us to come to it for universal knowledge. What Doctor Sampey writes of one book may be said of the whole Bible: It is "a book of *religious* fundamentals. Written at a period long prior to modern scientific research, it is not designed to take the place of such research. It uses the language of appearance and everyday life. Scientific precision was not a part of the author's purpose, but rather to lay a broad and solid foundation for faith in God and obedience to His commands."

No man who seeks in the Bible the guidance it claims to give will be disappointed—*if he seeks in the right spirit.* Jesus' criticism of the Pharisees was not that they searched the Scriptures thinking that in them they would have eternal life, but because their search lacked the open eye and open heart. They saw only what they wanted to see, and refused the full guidance of the truth spoken there. For such men the Bible is not sure guidance. But let one come with his heart open to the Spirit and desiring to find God, not for the guidance of his intellect alone, but for the guidance of his heart and his will,—for that man there is no disappointment.

2. What revelation and inspiration would lead us to expect *experience confirms.* From the day of David, with his fragmentary Bible, until now this has been the song of experience:

"The law of the Lord is *perfect,* restoring the soul:
The testimony of the Lord is *sure,* making wise the simple.
The precepts of the Lord are *right,* rejoicing the heart:
The commandment of the Lord is *pure,* enlightening the eyes."

(1) From among the possible New Testament experiences and teachings that might be cited here, let us notice *what Peter and Paul say.* Of course the Scriptures they refer to are the Old Testament, but that, instead of turning the edge of what they say, rather sharpens it for us who have the New Testament. *Peter's* words are written under the conviction that in prophecy "men spake from God, being moved by the Holy Spirit," but the note of experience also breaks forth in those great words, "And we have the word of prophecy made more sure; whereunto ye do well that ye take heed, as unto *a lamp shining in a dark place,* until the day dawn, and the day-star arise in your hearts." (2 Peter 1: 19, ASV). These are evidently the words of a man who was describing his own experience.

Paul also was recording his experience when he wrote to Timothy: "Abide thou in the things which thou hast learned, and hast been assured of, knowing of whom thou hast learned them; and that from a babe thou hast known *the sacred writings which are able to make thee wise unto salvation through faith which is in Christ Jesus."* And he goes on to say, "Every scripture *inspired of God* is also *profitable for teaching,* for *reproof,* for *correction,* for *instruction which is in righteousness;* that the man of God *may be complete,* furnished completely unto every good work" (2 Tim. 3:14-17). Here we find Paul's faith concerning the function and purpose of the Bible in relation to the life of God's people. It leads to salvation, to life under the restraint and urge of righteous standards, to complete personality, and complete equipment for the service of God. Paul has no doubt about it, for such had been his experience. Those who try it find it a sure lamp for their feet, a sure light for their pathways.

(2) Is it a book of sure guidance? Another affirmative is found in *men's consciousness of God's inner voice and power as they search its pages.* Coleridge spoke for many when he said, "In the Bible there is more that finds me than I have experienced in all other books put together; *the words of the Bible find me* at greater depths of my being; and whatever finds me brings with it an irresistible evidence of its having proceeded from the Holy Spirit"; and Doctor Mullins also when he wrote, "The Bible tells us how to find God and by following its directions *we actually find him.* God comes into our life and we know beyond a peradventure that the Bible speaks to us truly about God." Thus the claims and promises of the Scriptures are verified by the manifold experience of fellowship with God, vital assurance of his grace, and conscious power to do his work in the world, as we proceed upon the faith that he has spoken to us in them. They are indeed God's word—the literary record of his revelation in creation, history, individual experience, in Jesus Christ and his redemptive work. It is his

Word of Inspiration, originated by his Spirit in the hearts of holy men, and given to the world to serve the ends of his redeeming grace.

REVIEW QUESTIONS

1. What is meant by the statement that the Bible is a book of religion? How many religions are taught in it?

2. How do you explain the Bible's disproportionate treatment of history and its silence concerning the evils of slavery?

3. What is meant by the statement that the Bible is a book of revelation? Does this conflict with the facts studied in Chapter One?

4. What two reasons are found in the Bible for holding that it is a book of revelation?

5. What is meant by progressive revelation? Give two examples of the gradualness of revelation.

6. What bearing does the fact of progressive revelation have upon (1) our study of the Bible, and (2) some moral difficulties in the Old Testament?

7. Does the progressiveness of revelation help in the matter of the relation of the Bible to scientific knowledge? How?

8. On what grounds would you say that the Bible is a book of sure guidance?

9. Does it offer guidance in every field of knowledge?

10. Give the gist of what David (Psalm 19), Peter (2 Peter 1: 19), and Paul (2 Tim. 3: 14-17) say about the Scriptures.

11. What in substance is the testimony of S. T. Coleridge and Doctor Mullins?

12. Give your own statement of why the Bible ought to be called the Word of God.

FOR THE BLACKBOARD

A Book of Religion and Revelation

I. A Book of Religion
1. The fact evident everywhere
2. Explains Bible treatment of history
3. A key to some of the Bible silences
4. The Bible a book of one religion

II. A Book of Revelation
1. The claims of the writers in many places concerning Old Testament; concerning New Testament
2. Testimony of the great themes and character of the teaching

III. A Book of Growing Light
1. God revealed himself and his truth gradually
2. Examples of the growing light
   (1) In the conception of God
   (2) In the idea of worship
   (3) In the idea of righteousness
3. The significance of the progressiveness of revelation
   (1) For the study of the Bible
   (2) With respect to moral difficulties of Old Testament examples
   (3) With respect to the relation of science and the Bible

IV. A Book of Sure Guidance
1. The nature of the Bible invites confidence. This in the field of the Bible's purpose; and conditional upon the spirit of the seeker
2. The testimony of experience
   (1) Scriptural examples
   (2) Extra-biblical testimony

CHAPTER THREE

THE BOOK OF HEBREW HISTORY

In a literary classification of the Old Testament writings history occupies a large place. Much of the Pentateuch, Joshua, Judges, Ruth, Samuel, Kings, Chronicles, Esther, Ezra, Nehemiah, and large portions of the prophetical books, are to be classified as historical. Are these sections therefore to be passed over as of secondary importance, or read merely for the thrilling stories they tell of ancient peoples? Far from it! "One studies history," says Dr. F. K. Sanders, "to better understand the world he lives in, to acquaint himself with the achievements of men and with their mistakes, to catch the ideals of the best and greatest and to avoid the errors of the unworthy. History is not the satisfaction of curiosity, but the equipment for intelligent, efficient serviceableness to one's own generation." Such is the importance of the Old Testament history.

But there are other facts that give it unusual importance. It tells the story of the Hebrew nation, the people of our Saviour. It records the providential preparation of the world for his coming. It lays before our eyes the wonderful way in which God made himself known to men through their experiences. It records God's work through the centuries,—his creative work, his providential work, his redemptive work,—revealing himself as Power and Holiness and Love. If, therefore, we would enlarge our own understanding of God, and be able as teachers to make him real to others, these historical portions of the Bible are of the greatest value.

As an introduction and guide to a closer study of the subject let us seek the answer to three important questions: (1) What are the characteristics of the Old Testament history? (2) Who are the principal peoples of that history? And (3) what are the great epochs that stand out in its course?

I. Characteristics of the History

1. It is not *a universal history.* We must not expect to find here a history of the world. It follows one branch of the spreading tree of human experience. It begins at the point where all history has its beginning —the creation of the world (Gen. 1:2), but after a few sweeping descriptions of the experiences and expansion of the race (Gen. 3: 1-6: 8), and its new beginning in the sons of Noah (Gen. 6: 9-11: 10), it centers upon one of the sons, Shem, and his descendants (Gen. 11: 10-32). And again very quickly the story narrows to Abram (Gen. 12), then to Isaac (Gen. 21), and finally to Jacob and his family (Gen. 27), where the center of interest remains. Other peoples, the politically dominant peoples as well as the weaker, are either on the margin as touching in one way or another the life of Israel, or are not mentioned at all.

2. It is *not even a complete history of Israel.* To the ordinary historian its various records are very disproportionate to the values. Compare the space given to Abraham, Jacob, Joseph, and David and to the two Jeroboams, Omri, Ahab, Uzziah, and Hezekiah. These latter lived in stirring times when economic and political matters were pressing, and international relations claimed much attention. But no long descriptive documents find their way into the Bible, and what is there treats the political and economic as secondary. David, who reigned forty years, gets half of First Samuel and all of Second Samuel; Asa reigned forty-one years, and gets with his contemporaries in the North a couple of pages in Kings and as much in Chronicles. Many things no doubt happened in Asa's reign which would be most interesting and valuable in a study of social, economic, or political history, but they are not recorded. That

is to say, this is selected history; its materials were selected for a purpose.

3. What was *the principle of selection?* What was the purpose of the writers? The answer is, *religion.* These chapters record those events (1) which traced the religious growth of Israel and (2) whose record would influence men by warning or by encouragement to be true to God. Moved by the Spirit of God, the writers were concerned to write history that would reveal the deeper currents of life, the basic facts of individual and national experience, and the way to righteousness and fellowship with the Eternal. Other aspects of life are not denied, and are not denied their importance, but *the spiritual is presented as the determinative factor in history.* Political history is partial; so also is economic history or social history; so also is religious history, but it deals with that part of experience that means the strength or weakness, the progress or decay of the whole social structure and life.

This purpose explains not only the fragmentariness and seeming disproportion of the narratives, but also why the good and bad, the successes and failures of the nation, are recorded with equal faithfulness. Falsehood in Abraham, deceit in Jacob, adultery in David, despondency in Elijah, are exposed as simply and unapologetically as are their most laudable qualities.

4. A fourth characteristic is that *it conceives God to be the active cause behind all history.* Paul had the point of view of the history-writing prophets when he said that God "made of one every nation of men to dwell on the face of the earth, having determined their appointed seasons, and the bounds of their habitation" (Acts 17: 26, ASV). It was God who chose Abram, Jacob, and the nation of Israel; it was he who through the centuries steered the course of the nation in storm and darkness, through valleys and over mountains, on toward the goal of his great purpose.

So completely did this faith possess the historians that they spoke of God as raising up the enemies of Israel (see the Book of Judges and the period of Assyria's invasions) to punish the nation for its sin. He uses a Sennacherib to send away into captivity and a Cyrus to restore. He also punishes the other nations for their sins. God is the active power behind history. (See Deut. 4:32-40.) *Not economic conditions, not genius in statecraft, not the accident of fortune, nor the dead laws of social change, but God himself is the true explanation of history.* This is the Old Testament historians' philosophy of history. And by it we understand why they do not explain events in terms of economic or political aims, but in terms of the will of God. Secular historians say that the Assyrians and Egyptians, for instance, were moved by political motives to invade Palestine, and documentary facts support them. The Hebrew historian says the same invasions were judgments of God, never stopping with the secondary social causes in their explanation, and often omitting them altogether. They say to us that *we can never understand history until we have seen it in its reference to God.* And none can deny that they, too, speak the truth, and at a deeper level of reality than the secular historian.

5. Still another characteristic of this history is that it is written on *a framework of great characters.* For example, recall the great names of Abraham, Isaac, Jacob, Joseph, Moses, Joshua, Gideon, Samuel, David, and Elijah, to proceed no further along the course of the history. The heroism, insight, and convictions of these and others marked out the path of national experience and national faith. "To a unique degree, this is a history of dominating personalities." But the glory of these great men is that they are dominated by God. They kept alive the sense of divine mission, of the presence of God, of the goodness and wisdom of obedience. And their stories not only simplify and make more interesting the ancient narratives, but con-

stantly remind us that God relates himself to history through men, that he needs men, and raises them up to serve him.

II. The Principal Peoples of the History

Our study of Old Testament history will be greatly helped, both in point of interest and understanding, if we know something beforehand concerning the peoples whose experiences are the vehicles of its great truths.

1. *The central people* of the Old Testament are known by three names: *Hebrews,* after Abraham, who was called "the Hebrew," or "Crosser," presumably because he crossed over from Mesopotamia to Canaan; *Israelites,* because they were descendants of Jacob, also called Israel; and *Jews,* a term applied to them after the Exile, and having reference to Judea, their home. They belonged to the Semitic family, being descendants of Shem, one of the three sons of Noah. Of the same race were the Assyrians, and the Babylonians, the center of whose civilization was Ur, the early home of Abraham. About 2000 B.C. Abraham moved from Ur to Canaan (Palestine), which became the home of the Hebrew nation.

The Hebrews were characterized by *insight.* They were possessed of a practical insight which made them shrewd in their dealings and a practical wisdom that gave to their nation a remarkable persistence and stability through many centuries in the midst of much more powerful peoples. They were *not a warlike people.* Although they had many wars, their ideals were not those of empire. Their armies and fortifications existed only for defense and national security. Their statecraft was that of a peaceable people content to dwell in their own little land.

They were above all *a religious people.* And their religion they did not attribute to any religious genius, comparable to the philosophic and artistic genius of the Greeks, or the imperialistic genius of the Romans.

but to the fact that God chose to reveal himself to them. Inseparable from their religion was their *sense of mission.* Although they misread the way in which it would be accomplished, *they never doubted that they were chosen and set for the blessing of all nations, that through them God would establish his name in all the world.* They looked for a universal empire of righteousness. They were a people uniquely endowed and uniquely consecrated to a religious end. To be sure they displayed now and again a tragic fickleness which brought successive disasters upon the nation, but always there continued a remnant in whose hearts lived the high sense of mission and an unswerving faith in God.

2. *The Babylonians and Assyrians* are also prominent in the Old Testament story. They are mentioned together because they were the successive rulers in the same general territory, the Euphrates-Tigris valley, from which Abraham came. In the time of Abraham Hammurabi (Amraphel of Gen. 14: 9) was the ruler, and Babylon, his capital, was the center of the empire. The Bible does not follow the story of Babylonia, but by the time the people of Israel were delivered from Egypt, a province of the empire, Asshur (Assyria), located north of Babylon, had become an independent nation rivaling Babylonia. It is this Assyrian empire that in competition with Egypt harassed the Hebrew nation throughout much of its history. It was an Assyrian army that captured Samaria and led the northern tribes into exile in 722 B.C. About a century after that Babylonia was again in the ascendency, and it was a king of the new Babylon, Nebuchadnezzar, who destroyed Jerusalem in 587 B.C. Before the end of that century Babylonia had been conquered by Cyrus, who established the great Medo-Persian empire; and it was by his authority that the Jews returned to their land to renew their national life.

Although racially of the same stock as Israel, the Babylonians and Assyrians were very different. In religion they were polytheists and idolaters. They were militaristic, and depended for their wealth and progress upon conquest. Their respective nations built up great materialistic civilizations, but living by war their rule was always in peril through insurrection.

3. *The Egyptians,* whose land lay to the south of Canaan and was enriched by the great river Nile, also occupy a conspicuous place in Old Testament history. Abraham went to Egypt to escape famine. Joseph was sold into Egyptian slavery and later, when he had become prime minister, brought the whole family of his father Jacob thither (Gen. 37-50). Egypt thus became the home of the Hebrew people, where they remained for about four centuries until the time of Moses.

The Egyptians were the imperial rivals of the great eastern nations and contended with them for the domination of Palestine, which lay between and was commercially very important. Thus the land of the Hebrews was never free for long from the pressure from one or the other, and Egypt's name will be found a number of times in the course of the history, sometimes as friend and again as enemy. Israel's position was very much like that of Belgium or the Balkan States among the great European powers.

4. *Other peoples* found in the Old Testament history are the *Syrians,* to the northeast; the *Phœnicians,* to the northwest; the *Philistines,* to the southwest; and various smaller groups like the *Canaanites,* the *Moabites, Edomites, Ammonites,* and so forth, who were neighbors. These weaker peoples were, many of them, racially kindred, but differed in their religious faith and moral and social ideals. Politically they were always a problem; religiously their influence was a constant menace which prolonged until the Exile the battle of the prophets against idolatry in Israel. It was also the influence of these neighboring peoples that

made more difficult the moral progress of the common people.

III. The Course of the History

Other training course books will deal thoroughly with the details of the history. The purpose here is only to prepare for that study by giving a brief outline of the historical movement that can be easily held in mind. The importance of being able to think through the whole range of the history hardly needs arguing. Can we understand a hand apart from the body? Neither can we get the true significance of a period, or person, or event, or teaching unless we are familiar with the whole movement of which each is a part, and know at what point in that movement each appeared. Here, therefore, we must not despise memorizing.

1. Introduction

(Genesis 1-12: 3)

The first eleven chapters of Genesis are an introduction to the entire Bible. "They express in simple yet dignified and impressive fashion the religious ideas which every one must have in mind who reads the Old Testament with intelligent reverence" (F. K. Sanders). Now what are the great facts in this introduction?

(1) God created the universe, including man, whom he created in his own image and for dominion and fellowship with himself. (2) By sin man lost his first estate, introducing into life banishment, suffering, and death. (3) God did not accept man's defeat as final, but promised a future victory of mankind over the tempter. (4) God himself moved toward that redemption in judgment and mercy, destroying the race, but saving a righteous family for a new beginning. (5) Among the descendants of Noah, God chose Abraham (Abram), revealing himself especially to him in order to make him a blessing to all mankind.

2. THE PERIOD OF THE PATRIARCHS

(Genesis 12-50)

This period covered between three and four centuries, beginning about 2000 B.C. It began with Abraham in Ur of the Chaldees and ended with the great host in Egypt. The four principal figures were Abraham, Isaac, Jacob, and Joseph.

(1) *Abraham* (called Abram at the first) was born in Ur of the Chaldees, but at the call of God went out "not knowing whither he went." He journeyed to the North with his family, stopping first at Haran in Mesopotamia. After the death of his father, he, with his wife and his nephew, Lot, together with their households and possessions, journeyed on to the land of Canaan. There he pitched his tents, and, with the exception of brief periods in Egypt and Philistia, lived out his rich, worshipful life among its southern hills. He had two sons of biblical importance, Ishmael, the son of Hagar, and Isaac, the son of his wife Sarah. Isaac was the son whom God had promised beforehand, and who received the blessing of the first-born, becoming the heir of the promise which God had made to Abraham.

(2) The story of *Isaac* is brief and reveals him to have been a quiet, peace-loving man, without personal initiative, but persistent and faithful. His chief claim to honor lies in his blameless character, his inheritance of the promise, and his son Jacob.

(3) *Jacob* was the younger of twins, his brother being Esau. His story is one of the most human of all the biblical stories (Gen. 25ff). In his early life he was "Jacob," which means "supplanter." He later became "Israel," which means "prince of God." He amassed great wealth in sheep and cattle. He became the father of twelve sons, and they in turn became the fathers of the tribes of Israel.

(4) *Joseph* was the favorite son of Jacob. When still a boy his brothers, who hated him, sold him into

slavery. He became the slave of an Egyptian nobleman, and later, through the providence of God, the prime minister of that great state. In the midst of great famine he was instrumental in the removal of the whole family of his father Jacob and his brothers' families from Canaan to a rich section of Egypt. During his lifetime and long afterward the Israelites prospered there, and multiplied until they became a great nation. For a long time after Joseph's death there seems to have been no one outstanding leader, but they kept up their tribal or family organization, cherished their religion, and dreamed of a return to Canaan.

3. THE EXODUS AND SETTLEMENT IN CANAAN

(Exodus; Leviticus; Numbers; Deuteronomy; Joshua)

This brief period, covering strictly only about a half century, and less than a century if we include the whole of Joshua's life, is of great importance. Three geographical names stand out: Egypt, Mt. Sinai, and Canaan. There are also in the forefront three great personalities: Moses, Aaron, and Joshua.

(1) *Moses* is revered as the greatest of Israel's leaders, the emancipator and lawgiver. Born of Hebrew parents, reared and educated as a prince in the Egyptian court, he became the champion of his people in the midst of a great oppression which had descended upon them. Called and empowered by God he forced Pharaoh, through a series of divinely sent plagues, to set the Israelites free. He led them through the wilderness, and after nearly forty years gathered them in the plains of Moab, whence after his death they entered the Promised Land. In the wilderness at Mt. Sinai he received from God the Law—moral, ceremonial, and judicial,—which should be the basis of their national life in Canaan.

(2) *Aaron,* Moses' brother, was his mouthpiece before Pharaoh, and performed a service often underestimated. He was guilty of failing God and the people in the great idolatry at Mt. Sinai. But his essen-

tial goodness, and worth, are reflected in the fact that he was made the high priest in the ceremonial system that was erected, and had access to the most holy place on behalf of the people.

(3) *Joshua* was the military leader and the successor of Moses. In seven and a half years he overran the land of Canaan, and made it possible for the tribes to settle in the homes which they would hold through the centuries. In addition to his military service, Joshua kept alive the spiritual ideals of Israel, and led them to a renewal of their faith in God. The close of his life finds the nation settled, but without a strong leader able to hold the Twelve Tribes together in one government. And with bitter sufferings in store the nation faces the future.

4. THE DARK AGES

(Book of Judges; Ruth; 1 Samuel 1-7)

For perhaps three centuries the nation struggled on toward unity and autonomy. Beset by marauding neighbors from without, such as the Philistines, Moabites, and Midianites, they depended on "judges" to rally the tribes to self-defense. The moral problems within were just as great, and it seemed that the faith of Israel would perish. But God was faithful, and here and there were pious souls, and now and again a pious leader like Gideon turned the people back to him. At the close of the period came Samuel, one of the greatest of the prophets, in whose day the nation found its unity and power.

5. THE PERIOD OF THE UNITED KINGDOM

(1 Samuel 8-31; 2 Samuel; 1 Kings 1-11; 1 Chron. 10 to 2 Chron. 9)

Through the instrumentality of Samuel, *Saul,* the first king of Israel, was chosen. In his career the unique purpose of God for Israel and the religious demands upon the ruler were emphasized. He was counted a failure and his rejection announced by Samuel, not because he failed politically or on the field of battle, but because he failed morally and spiritually.

David, therefore, was chosen because he was "a man after God's own heart." Under David's rule the kingdom was expanded to its farthest limits, religion was made central, the people united, and God revealed through his prophets that David's throne should endure, and a Son of David would sit upon the throne forever.

Solomon came to the throne inspired by David's religious zeal. He built the Temple that David wanted to build, and made the national worship glorious. He was also noted for his practical wisdom and statecraft. He made politically advantageous alliances. He brought his kingdom to its highest point of wealth and splendor. But again the hand of God is seen in judgment,—for spiritual ideals were sacrificed for splendor, worship was compromised by idolatry, morality gave way to profligacy. Solomon forgot God and the people. He pressed them down by heavy tribute. He destroyed the unity which David had built up. And upon his death the kingdom was divided,—when it was only 120 years old.

6. THE PERIOD OF THE TWO KINGDOMS (931-587 B.C.)

(1 Kings 12-22; 2 Kings 1:1-24:9; 2 Chron. 10:1-36:16)

Solomon's son Rehoboam precipitated a rebellion that split the kingdom in two, and henceforth we must speak of two kingdoms: Israel and Judah. Israel, the Northern Kingdom, continued until 722 B.C., when its capital, Samaria, was captured by the Assyrians, and many of the people carried away captive. Judah continued until the destruction of Jerusalem and the captivity at the hands of Nebuchadnezzar (587 B.C.).

Politically this period was one of many wars. For a half century there was strife between the two kingdoms. There was war between Israel and Moab and Syria. The shadow of the Assyrian began to fall across the West and the kings of Israel and Judah sought security now in various alliances and again by paying tribute. From the middle of the ninth century on they were never at ease except when domestic problems kept the Assyrian armies at home. In these periods of quiet and favorable alliance both Israel and Judah showed great material progress. Assyria, however, was bent upon the domination of the West, and to that end destroyed the Northern Kingdom. And the survival of Judah for 135 years longer was not without the recurring menace which ripened into disaster in 587 B.C.

Religiously and morally it was also a period of alternating decline and revival. It is the great prophetic period. The prophets from Elijah to Jeremiah, without political offices, were God's ambassadors who sought to keep alive true faith and worship, and to preserve righteousness and justice. The next chapter will be devoted to their work. They were the saviors of religion and morality in the critical periods. It was they who interpreted the political experiences, connecting them with the sinfulness, the idolatry and moral corruption of the nation. They saw in Assyria and Babylonia the scourge of God. They interpreted alliances with Syria and Egypt as lack of faith in God. They foresaw and predicted the Exile as the inevitable outcome of persistent faithlessness.

7. THE PERIOD OF EXILE (605-535 B.C.)

(2 Kings 24:10-25:30; 2 Chron. 36:17-23; Esther; Parts of Jeremiah, Ezekiel, and Daniel)

For about seventy years the nation was homeless. To be sure the conquerors sought to preserve a semblance of national life by appointing a governor, but the flower of the nation was in captivity; the city and Temple destroyed; and soon many of those who were left fled to Egypt, taking the prophet Jeremiah with them. In Babylon the nation survived. Under the example of men like Daniel and his friends, and under the preaching of Ezekiel, the writings of Jeremiah, and the inspiration of the great promise of Isaiah 40-66, there was a purification and revival of religion. And from Ezra we gather that the Sacred Writings, also, were cherished and collected for use as they had not been before.

8. THE RESTORATION

(Ezra; Nehemiah)

Cyrus in reversing the deportation policy of the Babylonians and permitting the Jews to return, was chosen of God for carrying out his purpose for his people. Under Zerubbabel (535 B.C.), Ezra (458 B.C.), and Nehemiah (445 B.C.), the return and the restoration of Jerusalem and the Temple were accomplished. God's people entered into a new period of religious and political experiences. After Malachi no prophetic voice was heard until John the Baptist, the forerunner of the promised Messiah and Saviour.

REVIEW QUESTIONS

1. What is the importance of Old Testament history?

2. Name the five characteristics of Old Testament history.

3. On what principle was the material of the Bible selected? Compare its value with that of political, or economic history.

4. What was the Old Testament historian's idea of the relation of God to history? Give illustration.

5. Name twelve great personalities among the Hebrews in their historical order.

6. Give a general description of the Hebrew people.

7. Write a sentence or two about each of the other leading peoples of the Old Testament.

8. Give the general outline of Hebrew history (eight points).

9. What great facts are brought out in the Introduction to Hebrew history?

10. Outline the period of the "Exodus and Settlement in Canaan."

11. Describe the course of things during the "Period of the Two Kingdoms," politically, religiously, and morally.

12. Give the most important facts concerning the "Period of Exile."

FOR THE BLACKBOARD

The Book of Hebrew History

I. Characteristics of the History
   1. Not universal history
   2. Not a complete history of the Hebrews
   3. History from the standpoint of religion
   4. Conceives God to be the active cause behind all history
   5. Written on a framework of great biographies

II. The Principal Peoples of the History
   1. The central people: Hebrews—Israelites—Jews, characterized by insight, religion, sense of mission
   2. The Babylonians and Assyrians
   3. The Egyptians
   4. Other peoples of the Old Testament

III. The Course of the History
   1. Introduction. Significance of Genesis 1-12
   2. The Period of the Patriarchs
      Abraham—Isaac—Jacob—Joseph
   3. The Exodus and settlement in Canaan
      Moses—Aaron—Joshua
   4. The Dark Ages. Duration and significance of the period
   5. The Period of the United Kingdom
      Saul—David—Solomon
   6. The Period of the Two Kingdoms
      Israel and Judah. Political, moral and religious features
   7. The Period of the Exile
   8. The Restoration

CHAPTER FOUR

THE BOOK OF HEBREW PROPHECY

Hebrew history cannot be understood apart from Hebrew prophecy. The sketch of the history in its external framework given in the last chapter must remain not unlike other histories until we see the prophet in the midst. We must hear his interpretation of the nation's experience, his arraignment of the people, including priests and kings, for their sins, and his challenge to righteousness and holiness; we must feel the impact of his preaching upon the political, moral, and religious life of the nation before we can mark the difference between Israel and Assyria, or Egypt or Greece. We only separate the two in study in order to emphasize the place and importance of each in the working out of God's purpose in Israel.

Several questions present themselves: What is meant by "prophet" and "prophecy"? What were the characteristics of true prophets? How did they differ from the priests and the rulers? What was the nature of their service to Israel? What actual contributions did they make to the life of their nation and to the world?

1. The Prophet and His Mission

1. The Hebrew prophet was *one who spoke for God to men.* He was God's man and his message was God's message. He entered upon this service neither by inheritance nor popular choice, but by a *special call from God.*

Examples of the prophetic call may be seen (1) in the words of Amos (7: 14-15, ASV), "I was no prophet, neither was I a prophet's son; but I was a herdsman, and a dresser of sycomore trees: and Jehovah took me from following the flock, and Jehovah said unto me, Go, prophesy unto my people Israel"; (2) in the words of Isaiah (6: 8-9, ASV), "I heard the voice of the Lord, saying, Whom shall I send, and who will go for us? Then I said, Here am I; send me. And he said, Go, and tell this people . . . "; and (3) in the words of Jeremiah (1: 4-10, ASV), "The word of Jehovah came unto me, saying, Before I formed thee in the belly I knew thee, and before thou camest forth out of the womb I sanctified thee; I have appointed thee a prophet unto the nations. . . . Behold, I have put my words in thy mouth." Thus it was no human ordination, but a divine appointment that sent the prophet forth. "He was no man pleaser, pandering to the passion of the masses or catering to the prejudices of the classes. He was the servant of Jehovah and spake in the fear of the Lord."

2. We must notice also the *personality and special gifts* of the prophets. They are not to be compared with microphones or phonographic records or robots. They were the most conscious, the most alert, the most dynamic personalities in Israel. Theirs was not the courage of the ignorant or the irresponsible, but the open-eyed courage of men of conviction.

(1) *They were men of insight.* They not only saw things, but the meaning of things. And they gave their attention to the things that had meaning. Joel read the meaning of the drought and the plague, and Isaiah discerned the way of victory over a threatening foe. Amos and Jeremiah read unerringly the signs of the times. They could see the web of facts that bound into one bundle public and private life, religion and business, politics and morality, and they knew what was cause and what effect. And they knew what the will of God was.

(2) *They were men of foresight.* Not only did they have the insight to judge and interpret; they had the

foresight to warn and predict. They were like *watchers on the wall* (Isa. 21:11-12; Ezek. 3:16) to warn of approaching disaster, or herald the dawn of a new day. Prediction is no longer thought of as the chief element in the prophets' ministry, but it was a real and authentic part; and its importance when we try to measure its gravity or its influence upon the religion of Israel, can hardly be exaggerated. They kept alive in the hearts of the people the great national hope based on the promise of God. But they did not fail, however, to see the shadows of judgment for sin. More than one of them predicted the Exile. One may say that any wise statesman might have done that, but it took a prophet to see the deeper reason for it and to see beyond the exile the day of restoration and triumph in the kingdom of the Messiah. The foresight of the prophet was a gift of God, and the messianic predictions are of greatest importance. (See Chapter Six.)

(3) Their insight and foresight were inseparable from *a great faith in God.* Paul was voicing the faith of the prophets when he wrote, "For of him, and through him, and unto him, are all things. To him be the glory for ever" (Rom. 11: 36, ASV). The *explanation of everything was in God.* Thus for Israel and for the world they were the *pioneers of faith,* each of them seeing and voicing the great fact about God that needed emphasis in his particular day. Moses emphasized the constancy, the covenant-keeping faithfulness of God; Elijah, the supremacy of God; Amos, the righteousness of God; Hosea, his love and mercy; Isaiah, his holiness; Jeremiah, his accessibility to the seeking soul anywhere. All of them believed in *God's purpose for Israel* and gave themselves to making the people see him and to leading them to obey him.

3. It is important also to notice *the range of the prophets' ministry.* In general it may be said that they were concerned with the whole life of Israel. Nothing that affected the spirit and purpose of the nation was

foreign to their interest. One's emphasis was upon social justice, another's upon God's judgment of the nations, one attacked political evils, another the corruption of worship, each according to his special divine guidance. But the ministry of the prophet was never limited to any segment or aspect of life, as was that of the priest. He was a watchman on the walls, seeing all and ministering in all.

(1) The prophets had an important *political ministry.* In Moses the prophet was the recognized ruler. Samuel anointed both Saul and David, and held a strong position with the chosen king. In a sense he was superior to the king. So also all the great prophets dared to rebuke kings, to condemn or to recommend political policies, to expose corruption in high places. Sometimes they were the accepted friendly *advisers* (compare Elisha and Jehu; Isaiah and Hezekiah): again they were hated as *trouble makers* (Elijah and Ahab; Amos and Jeroboam II). Always they contended for righteousness and justice in government.

(2) *Economic conditions received much attention also.* Hear, for example, Amos' indictment of the people of Israel: "They have sold the righteous for silver, and the needy for a pair of shoes—they that pant after the dust of the earth on the head of the poor, and turn aside the way of the meek" (2: 6f, ASV); or Isaiah's condemnation in Jerusalem of those who "join house to house," and "lay field to field" (Isa. 5: 8, ASV) in greediness, while the poor cry out under oppression. They are the *champions of the oppressed,* the *preachers of social justice.*

(3) Nor did the prophets fail to speak a clear and uncompromising message concerning *personal and private morals.* The moral precepts of the Decalogue were never forgotten. There was unceasing insistence upon ethical ideals to be expressed in sincere character and righteous conduct. If the nation was to be righteous in its political and economic and social life, then in-

dividuals must be righteous. Recall Samuel and Saul (1 Sam. 15: 12-23); Nathan and David (2 Sam. 12: 1-15); and such arraignments as those in Isaiah 5 and numerous other prophetic writings.

(4) The prophets, however, were more than moral and political reformers, as we use the terms today. Their central and ever-present interest was religion. *Worship, therefore, occupies them along with social conduct.* They can hardly find words with which to denounce false and insincere worship (Isa. 1:11-17). The acme of evil was for men to magnify their public worship while their hearts and hands were full of guilt unconfessed. To them ceremony meant nothing apart from sincere faith and clean lives. So vehement was their protest against meaningless worship that they seemed at times to be opposed to sacrifice and ceremony altogether.

Thus we see the broad field of the prophet's ministry. "All questions that involved righteousness and justice were his themes." He was political adviser or critic, the champion of the oppressed, moral reformer, ecclesiastical critic and reformer, the spokesman for God in every realm of life. He brought everything to the light and judgment of the character of God, the word of God, and the work of God as he revealed himself through his Spirit and providence.

4. A further word must be said about *the aim and method of the prophets.*

(1) The prophetic aim was, first, *to keep the people true to the ideals and truths of religion* that God had revealed to them. They were trying to keep religion and to keep it ethical. The temptation and tendency in Israel was to separate religion from morality, and so to lose both. The prophets sought to preserve both by bringing them together. Their aim was also, to quote Dr. J. R. Sampey, *"to pave the way for the future progress of the kingdom of God,"* which, according to

promise, was destined to rule over all humanity in righteousness.

(2) To such ends the *method* of the prophets was adapted. The method was fitted to the time and place and nature of the prophets' particular tasks. Sometimes they *delivered their counsel privately,* of which there are many examples in the dealing of the prophets with the rulers; again they *proclaimed their messages publicly* in the Temple court or in the streets, or other places of assembly. Most of the books of the prophets were thus delivered. They were pre-eminently preachers. For a wider and permanent service they wrote down, and often in poetical form, many of the messages they had preached, as our Scriptures testify. When so led by the Spirit of God their preaching sometimes became *dramatic and symbolic,* as for example in the case of Isaiah (compare Chaps. 8 and 13), Jeremiah (compare Chap. 19: 1-13), and Ezekiel (compare Chaps. 4, 5, 17, 37, and so forth). And in the case of some of the prophets, especially in the early days, their power and authority were vouchsafed by *special miracle.* Outstanding examples are found in Moses' work in Egypt and in the wilderness (Exodus), and in the ministries of Elijah and Elisha (1 Kings 17; 2 Kings 4).

II. The Story of the Prophets

To say that the history of Israel felt the power of such men as those described above, and that much of our Old Testament came to us by their hand, surely ought to quicken a desire to know more of them individually. When did they first appear in the life of the nation? Who were the greatest among them? Were they much alike, or did they differ widely in their personal qualities and temperaments? In what circumstances did their ministry become most notable?

1. *Before the Formation of the Kingdom*

(1) *The beginnings of prophecy* lie far back in human history. Enoch and Noah are spoken of in the

New Testament as prophesying (Jude 14f. and 2 Peter 2: 5). Abraham also is called a prophet (Gen. 20: 7). When one compares the character of the prophets and the nature of prophecy among the Hebrews from Abraham's time onward with the soothsaying, necromancy, and so forth, of other ancient people, he sees a difference that puts Hebrew prophecy in a class by itself. It bears the stamp of reality, as being not a natural development, but a supernatural manifestation. In its emotional aspects and its modes (such as ecstasy, dreams, visions) it often had much in common with "prophets" of other peoples, but in content, purpose, and character, as well as in its sure progress to higher levels, it was a different sort of thing. The great books of the prophets testify to the reality of prophecy from the very beginning of Hebrew history.

(2) *The high peak of early prophecy* was reached in Moses. Indeed, he was the greatest of all the prophets. It is said of him that he spoke "face to face" with God. Without the miracle of revelation and the reality of a special divine call and equipment, Moses is beyond explanation. He was raised up at the crisis of national birth, to lead the people to freedom, to give them laws, to organize their life, to guide in the selection of future tribal homes. The high dream of the nation was that in the future another prophet like him would appear.

(3) Around him and in the Period of the Judges were *other prophetic spirits.* Mention is made of the prophetic gifts of Miriam, Aaron, Joshua, and Deborah. Besides these we read of that curious character, Balaam, who showed how the Spirit of God can work through great imperfections (Num. 22-24). By the close of the Period of the Judges the spirit of prophecy was so widespread that a prophetic order appeared with Samuel as its leader.

2. *The Period of the United Kingdom*

(1) Here the name of *Samuel* stands out. Notice at this point what will be observable all along, that the

greater prophets appeared at the great crises of history. There were many prophets through the centuries, but those whose names we know, or whose writings we have, were God's men in critical times. Moses was raised up to establish the nation. Now Samuel is raised up to guide the nation in its transition from a loose tribal organization to a compact kingdom. Samuel anointed Saul (1 Sam. 9-10), and, as long as Saul would listen to him, was his counselor. When Saul's arrogance and disobedience to God revealed his unworthiness to be king, it was Samuel who announced his rejection and God's choice of another. He anointed David (1 Sam. 16) and then retired to Ramah where, it seems, he spent the brief remaining period of his life.

Besides his work in connection with the kingship, Samuel did two remarkable services—the one as judge of Israel and the other as leader of the "school of the prophets." As judge he traveled about the country from year to year counseling the people (1 Sam. 6: 15ff), and as prophetic leader he kindled and guided him as used of God to give character, spirit and di- the religious fires of young Israel. We may think of rection to the work of the prophets which will be so much needed in the complex and trying experiences of the next historical period.

(2) There were, besides Samuel and the young prophetic group, other prophets worthy of mention. Although *David* himself had prophetic gifts, he had by his side two true and courageous prophets, Gad and Nathan, who were invaluable counselors in matters of state, religion, and personal morality. *Gad* was with him in his flight from Saul (1 Sam. 22: 5) and was still his adviser near the close of his reign (2 Sam. 24: 11-19). *Nathan,* one of the noblest of prophets, was God's messenger to deliver to David that great messianic promise, "Thy house and thy kingdom shall be made sure for ever before thee; thy throne shall be established for ever" (2 Sam. 7: 16, ASV). It was he also who

confronted David with his great sin (2 Sam. 12), and was instrumental in obtaining the crown for Solomon (1 Kings 1).

3. *The Period of the Divided Kingdom*

This was the period of many crises and many prophets. There were periods of prosperity and moral crisis, and of depression and political crisis. There were *false prophets* who prophesied for a price (of money or favor); *weak prophets,* who, drifting with the tides with good intention and missing the divine message, were false without knowing it; and there were strong and *true prophets* whose names we hold in highest honor because they spoke from God.

(1) The first group of these last we may call *the non-writing prophets, i. e.,* prophets whose writings do not appear in the Old Testament, although some of them probably were writers (compare Iddo and Jehu, 2 Chr. 12: 15; 13: 22; 20: 34). How many of these there were we do not know. In 1 Kings 11-20; 2 Kings 2-8, and 2 Chr. 12-20 fourteen are mentioned by name or deed, and an indefinite number referred to. Among them is *Ahijah,* the Shilonite, who announced to Jeroboam that because of the sin of the people God would rend the kingdom and give to him ten tribes (1 Kings 11: 29ff), and who later on, because of Jeroboam's sin, announced that God would take the kingdom (Israel) away from his house and give it to another.

The greatest names among them are Elijah and Elisha. Both of them lived in stirring times and were great powers in the Northern Kingdom (Israel). *Elijah* appeared at a time when the very religion of Israel was in the balance. Jezebel, wife of King Ahab, had introduced Baal worship and become militant in her effort to substitute it for the worship of Jehovah. The stern prophet challenged the whole movement and brought it to the test on Mt. Carmel where the reality of Jehovah was proved and the people brought back from their idolatry (1 Kings 17-18). Afterwards he continued his ministry through the reign of Ahab and his son, denouncing sin and voicing the judgment and will of God. His successor, *Elisha,* a man of gentler spirit, carried on the work of his stern teacher with unflinching courage. His ministry was one of mingled severity and gentleness (2 Kings 2-8), made beautiful by his gentle service to the poor widow and the raising of the Shunammite's son.

(2) A second group of prophets in this period is composed of *the writing (canonical) prophets.* Their books occupy a large part of the Old Testament. A volume might be written about each one of them. Let us only try to get a swiftly-moving picture of their ministry, as represented in a few of the greater ones.

In the Northern Kingdom the name *Amos* stands out. Elisha had not been dead many years before Amos was born. He grew up in a time of material prosperity and religious depression. Idolatry, immorality, oppression, and greed abounded, and Amos with unbending courage preached the righteousness of God, announcing the judgment of God not only upon Israel, but Judah also, and the nations round about. A contemporary of his was *Hosea,* whose spirit was one of sorrow rather than indignation, a man who out of his own personal suffering preached to Israel the continuing love of God in their unfaithfulness, and his willingness to forgive and redeem. Other prophets of the North were *Obadiah, Joel,* and *Jonah.* The preaching of these faithful men did not avail, and in 722 B.C., when the echo of Hosea's words (740 B.C.) still rang, Israel was overthrown by the Assyrians.

In the Southern Kingdom (Judah) the two great names are Isaiah and Jeremiah. *Isaiah* is often called the prince of the prophets. He was a youth when the glory of King Uzziah faded and the Assyrian war clouds were on the horizon. The Northern Kingdom was rapidly declining, and old and young in Judah were in the grip of a great fear. In the year of Uzziah's death young Isaiah saw his vision of God upon his throne, and gave himself at God's call to be his prophet (Isaiah 6). And for forty years he preached and wrought with a consecration and spiritual power unexcelled. His book portrays a zeal, a prophetic insight and foresight, an energy, a statesmanship, an eloquence, a courage, a devotion to God and his fellow man, that put him among the great of all ages. He sought by counsel with Ahaz (Isaiah 7), and again with Hezekiah (Isaiah 36-39) to shape the political policies of Judah in accordance with the will of God. With the passion of an Amos and the pathos of a Hosea he denounced sin and pleaded with the people to repent. He warned against judgment, predicting the exile of the nation, of Judah along with Israel, if the people did not repent. He pictured in highest eloquence the glorious purpose of God to establish his kingdom forever and to raise up his Anointed One to be the ruler of the nations.

In *Jeremiah* we have a picture of the true prophet when his world is collapsing about him. Like Isaiah, he saw the inevitableness of the Captivity. The difference was that he saw the enemy at the very gates. What could he do? He did several things. He loved his people and took their sorrows upon his own heart. In order to save them from unnecessary suffering he counseled immediate surrender of Jerusalem to the Babylonians, for which he came near to losing his life. He was made to suffer as a traitor. Another thing he did was to proclaim the connection between the captivity and the sinfulness and idolatry of the people. He also preached the faithfulness of God still to keep his promise to redeem his people. Captivity came and his faith held firm. He continued to minister in suffering and against great odds to those who with him remained in Judah, until he was forcibly carried away into Egypt.

4. *The Period of the Exile*

Here the name of *Jeremiah* must be mentioned again, for it was he who wrote to the exiles assuring them that they could worship God acceptably without the Temple or the altar. He preached the true spirituality of religion. He also preached the individuality of religion, that a man's fellowship with God is not dependent upon the success of the nation. The meaning of that ministry to a people who had been so confident of national safety and so dependent upon ritual cannot be measured.

Here, too, must be mentioned the great Book of Comfort, Isaiah, (40-66) which was to the exiles a breath from heaven, to turn men's hearts to the future and create a new faith in the Redeemer, whose own sufferings will be the price of their healing, and whose glorious power will be their hope of eternal salvation.

Two other prophets of the Exile were Ezekiel and Daniel. *Ezekiel* was the prophet of reconstruction. He lived very close to the people as their pastor and teacher. He spoke even more emphatically than Jeremiah of individual responsibility and hope. He taught in sermon and symbol the resurrection of the nation and new life in the old home. *Daniel* lived a life of great moral beauty and must have greatly influenced many of his own people who otherwise might have been led to desert the worship of God in that strange land. He, too, looked forward to the Restoration and the glories of the Messianic Age.

5. *After the Restoration* the work of rebuilding the Temple and the city of Jerusalem was set forward by the prophetic voices of *Haggai* and *Zechariah;* and *Malachi,* the last of the prophets, until John the Baptist, lifted up his voice against newly encroaching social evils, the temptation in the difficult times to offer worthless sacrifices, and the tendency to be skeptical concerning the promises and purposes of God. These words from Malachi may well be read as representing

the gospel of the prophets in every age: "Unto you that fear my name shall the sun of righteousness arise with healing in its wings" (Malachi 4: 2, ASV). The prophets saw the day of Christ and the promise of his coming was always the basis of their optimism.

REVIEW QUESTIONS

1. What is meant by "prophet" and "prophecy"?

2. Give examples of the call of the prophet as told by Amos, Isaiah, and Jeremiah.

3. Discuss the three outstanding characteristics of the true prophet.

4. Describe the range of the prophets' interest and ministry. Tell something of their political ministry.

5. What was the aim of the prophet? What methods did he use in his work?

6. Who were the earliest prophetic voices mentioned in the Bible? What was the high peak of early Hebrew prophecy?

7. Who was the next outstanding prophet after Moses? Tell something of his ministry.

8. What three kinds of prophets are found in the Period of the Two Kingdoms? How are the true prophets classified?

9. Who were the principal prophets of the Northern Kingdom? Of the Southern Kingdom?

10. Tell something of the life and work of Isaiah.

11. Tell something of the life and work of Jeremiah.

12. Tell something of the ministry of the prophets of the Exile.

FOR THE BLACKBOARD

The Book of Hebrew Prophecy

Relation of Prophecy to History

I. The Prophet and His Mission

1. The prophet was one called of God to speak to men for him
   Examples of the prophetic call

2. Personality and special gifts of the prophets
   (1) Men of insight. Interpreters
   (2) Men of foresight. Watchers
   (3) Men of great faith in God. The Messianic hope
3. The range of the prophets' ministry
   (1) Political ministry. Examples
   (2) Ministry in economic field. Social morality
   (3) Personal and private morals taught. Examples
   (4) Message concerning worship
4. The aim and method of the prophets
   (1) The aim
   (2) Method adapted to ends
   Private counsel. Public proclamation. Dramatic action. Miracle

II. The Story of the Prophets
1. Before the formation of the Kingdom
   (1) The beginnings of prophecy
   (2) The high peak of early prophecy. Moses. Others after him
2. The Period of the United Kingdom
   (1) Samuel
   (2) David, Gad and Nathan
3. The period of the Divided Kingdom
   Three kinds of prophets: false; weak; true
   (1) The non-writing prophets: Ahijah, Elijah, Elisha
   (2) The writing prophets
   In the Northern Kingdom: Amos, Hosea
   In the Southern Kingdom: Isaiah, Jeremiah
4. The Period of the Exile
   Jeremiah, Isaiah (40-66), Ezekiel, Daniel
5. After the Restoration
   Haggai, Zechariah, Malachi

CHAPTER FIVE

THE BOOK OF HEBREW WORSHIP AND WISDOM

Besides history and prophecy there remain two aspects of Hebrew life, which were of great importance in the development of the people and their contribution to our own religious life. One of these is *worship*. From the earliest chapters of Genesis we find present the two elements of all true worship—God's approach to man in self-revelation, and man's approach to God in sacrifice, prayer, and so forth. In this Old Testament story of worship we have an invaluable insight into the qualities that make devotional life true and satisfying. In following it we have for our guidance the ceremonial law, the worship practices of the people, the message of the prophets concerning worship, and the great Book of Psalms.

The other aspect of life finds its chief expression in what is called the Wisdom Books—Job, Ecclesiastes, and Proverbs. It is the *intellectual grappling with the experiences, problems, and ends of life*. It has been said that the Hebrews were not a speculative people, but that does not mean that they sensed no intellectual problems connected with the high teachings of the prophets concerning revelation, providence, and the place of religion in life. The Hebrews were not a passive people. Tradition and revelation found alert minds who brought them to the test of thought and experience. We must study the Old Testament therefore as a book of worship and wisdom.

I. A Book of Worship

1. *The beginnings of worship* lie back near the beginning of human life. The first recorded act of

worship was that of Cain and Abel, when they brought each "an offering unto Jehovah." No explanation is given of the ideas or motives which prompted them, but we know they sought the favor and fellowship of God.

In Genesis 8: 20, ASV, we read that immediately after the flood subsided "Noah builded an altar unto Jehovah, and took of every clean beast, and of every clean bird, and offered burnt offerings on the altar." In Genesis 12:7 and subsequent passages we learn that it was the custom of Abraham to build wherever he lived an altar unto God. So at its beginning the Hebrew race had its simple ceremonies of worship—altar and offerings—in which under the leadership of the patriarch the household sought the favor and fellowship of God.

2. *From the time of Moses* the customs of worship were given definite recognized forms in ceremonial laws. Not all the forms and meanings of worship were new with Moses; there had been a development in the hundreds of years since Abraham; but now they were given the objective sanction of God. We cannot here go into a description of that ceremonial system, nor discuss the extensiveness of it at the beginning. It is enough to notice that at the beginning of national life worship was exalted and given a definiteness of expression which put God at the center of it all. No royal dynasty was established, but a priestly tribe (Levi) was chosen, and the high priestly office committed to Aaron and his sons after him. Provision was made by which, if men were sincere, they might find forgiveness of their sins and find acceptance and fellowship in the covenant which God had made with the nation—that he would be their God and they would be his people forever.

3. Turning from the fact of the high importance and the most careful provision made for worship by the spiritual leaders of the Hebrews, let us inquire into *the worship practices of the people.* Were they true to

God and faithful in worship? Or was there a tendency to neglect or to pervert the sacred engagements? In the Bible the story is told in all frankness. The common practices were far from ideal. For one thing the people had a *lamentable weakness for idolatry*. Rachel stole her father's gods and brought them into Jacob's household (Gen. 31: 30-32) and Manasseh thirteen hundred years later "built altars for all the host of heaven in the two courts of the house of Jehovah . . . and he set the graven image of the idol, which he had made, in the house of God" (2 Chron. 33: 5, 7, ASV). The sin of idolatry was like an inky black stream running the full length of the history until it was purified during the Exile. In Palestine the Israelites were surrounded by idolatrous peoples. Their tribal neighbors within their own land also worshiped idols, while of their God there was no image or representation of any kind, and like multitudes in our modern world they yielded to the sense-attraction of the visible and the tangible. And in the Northern Kingdom Jeroboam capitalized this weakness by erecting the golden calves at Bethel and Dan, and further corrupted the worship by choosing others than Levites for priests. Thus Jeroboam gave a bent to worship in Israel that led away from truth and spirituality.

Furthermore, with the same spiritual blindness many saw no further than the ceremonies, which became sacraments, effective (so they thought) apart from the spirit of the worshiper. They became the whole of religion. And this *unreality* was a problem that not even the suffering of exile solved. Not only Isaiah, but Jesus also faced the mockery of unreality among people who were the most scrupulous ceremonialists.

4. Of great value in understanding the Old Testament life and ideals is *the attitude of the prophets toward worship* and the forms of worship. They *denounced the worship that was unreal* because of sin. Amos (4: 4, ASV) spoke with biting sarcasm: "Come to Beth-

el, and transgress; to Gilgal, and multiply transgression; and bring your sacrifices every morning, and your tithes every three days;" Isaiah declares that worship is an abomination to God when men go on in sin. A paragraph of intensest passion voicing the condemnation of God (1: 10-17, ASV) is full of the strongest statements: "When ye spread forth your hands (in prayer), I will hide mine eyes from you; yea, when ye make many prayers, I will not hear: your hands are full of blood." Through Hosea God says: "I desire goodness, and not sacrifice; and the knowledge of God more than burnt-offerings" (6: 6, ASV). It should be noted, however, that the prophets *were not hostile to ceremonial worship.* They were only hostile to making the sacrifices the end of worship, disregarding the will of God in the ordering of life.

As the years passed and the evils of false worship brought the nation nearer to spiritual collapse the prophets saw that worship is *essentially a personal matter* between a man and God, and not a ceremonial of and for the nation. Jeremiah and Ezekiel preached individual responsibility for sin, and necessarily therefore for worship—prayer and sacrifice, also. They also saw after the Captivity, when Temple and ritual were gone, that *apart from priest or altar or Temple, worship out of a pure and diligent heart will find God* (Jer. 29:13). Still they did not oppose the ceremonies and sacrifices, and when the nation was restored the remaining prophets encouraged the support of the Temple. But the prophets' vision led the way toward the attitude of Jesus who predicted the passing of sacred places with their systems as in the order of God.

5. We cannot know the depth and richness of the spirit of worship in the Old Testament apart from *the Psalms,* which were being written through the centuries alongside the history and the prophecies. The perversions and abuses of worship noted in the paragraphs above show only one side of the picture. From earliest

times music and song had a large place in Hebrew life. There were secular songs, of course; but there were many that centered in the religious experiences and aspirations of the people, songs which, upon the lips of individuals, were the outpouring of the hearts of men, women, and children in prayer and praise; and sung by the great temple choirs, accompanied by musical instruments, they voiced the deeper sentiments and hopes of the whole nation.

(1) The Psalms occupied in Israel the place our hymns occupy in the churches today. Many of them, like Matheson's great hymn, "O Love that wilt not let me go," were first the *spiritual utterances of individual souls* who had no thought of their being incorporated in a hymn book. Such, for example, were Psalms 23, 25, 51, 73, etc., where the personal experiences of the writer are unmistakable. Others, no less sincere, were written primarily to *express the common experiences and desires of the people* in collective worship. Such for the most part, were the songs of the sons of Korah, and Asaph (compare 42-49; 50: 74-83). Concerning the Book of Psalms as a whole F. R. Sanders writes: "It reflects the inner consciousness of Israel, but likewise of all godly souls. . . . The Psalter is the world's interpreter of God to man. God is its great reality. It seizes upon eternal things and interprets them to human need. Hence, mankind will use these 'praises of Israel' while the world stands."

(2) The Book of Psalms was a growth, added to from century to century out of the heart of Israel. The period of David, however, was especially rich in song. David was a musician, poet, and ardent worshiper of Jehovah, and himself wrote many psalms. In the superscriptions of the Psalms he is credited with seventy-three of the one hundred and fifty. Although these superscriptions were probably added after the songs began to be collected into hymn books, and are not always correct, they are not to be wholly dis-

credited. They credit one each to Moses (90) and Ethan (89); two to Solomon (72, 127); twelve to Asaph, a Levitical conductor of temple music; and twelve to the sons of Korah, a family of Levitical singers. In Jeremiah's day, a time of trial and fear, many prayer psalms seem to have been added. The Period of the Exile and after was also very active in the collection of psalms. So all through the nation's history pious musicians and poets were expressing to God, out of their own experience and sympathy, the deep longings of the people, and to the nation the glory and grace of God.

(3) In the worship of the Psalms *Israel expresses its faith.* In prayer and praise are revealed a great reverence and sense of dependence, a *belief in the power and goodness* of God who is a refuge and deliverer. *The hope of Israel* shines in the great Messianic psalms, in which prophecies concerning the King, the Kingdom, and the Suffering Servant are more than echoed (Psalms 2, 22, 72, 110, etc.). The Hebrew *conception of sin,* the need of forgiveness, the duty of confession, the grace of God in forgiveness and triumph all find expression in numberless places. There are portrayed also the *great qualities of a good life,* the "blessed" man, both in respect to personal character and the virtues of social conduct. The Psalms, therefore, are more than the musical adornments of ritual; they throb with spiritual emotion; they stir the soul to think high thoughts; they carry beyond the earthly scene into the heavenly presence of God. In them the two elements of worship are linked together: man approaches God and God approaches man, for they bear as clear a mark of inspiration as any part of the Scriptures. In them the worship of Israel was glorious, and served to keep alive the faith and hope that continued to glow until the day of Christ. This is a feature of the Old Testament—this emphasis upon pure and constant worship, both public and private,—that

the church today cannot neglect, except at the cost of decline and disaster.

II. A Book of Wisdom

Another distinct element of the Old Testament is portrayed in Job, Proverbs, and Ecclesiastes. They are not history, although Job has a historical background. Neither can they be classified as prophecy, although they have prophetic value. Their point of view and purpose are better described by the word "wisdom." They deal with the problems of life: problems that bear upon the traditional view of God and his dealings with men (Job); perplexities and disappointments that easily lead to skepticism and despair (Ecclesiastes); the practical problems of life in the home, in business, and society in general (Proverbs). Here we have the Old Testament's nearest approach to the "wisdom," the intellectual approach and method, of the Greeks. But where the Greeks speculated and theorized, these "wise men" reached practical conclusions on the basis of experience, observation of men, and their belief in God.

1. *Proverbs,* for example, is a book of practical wisdom about many things. It was completed probably in the time of Hezekiah (Prov. 25: 1). When the writing of proverbs began we do not know. It is said that "Solomon's wisdom excelled the wisdom of all the children of the East, and all the wisdom of Egypt," and that he spoke three thousand proverbs. There must have been many before his day, and many others were created later. So renowned was his reputation that many think he gave his name to a certain form of proverbial expression, which came to be "Solomonic proverbs"; and that this explains why the name of Solomon is attached to so many of those in this book. Possibly he wrote all that bear his name. But the proverbs rather than their particular author are our chief interest. What do they tell us about life?

(1) Notice first the *nature of a proverb.* Lord Russell described a proverb as "the wisdom of many and the wit of one." Another has said that it is *compressed experience:* "not one nor two but countless observations of men and things have gone to the making of a single proverb; it is the conclusion to which a thousand premises pointed the way; it is compressed experience." As such it is packed full of meaning. The writer just quoted advises on the basis of this fact that the proverbs yield greater results if we read few of them at a time and think long upon them. We cannot digest much of such strong food taken at once.

(2) What is *the purpose of the book?* Read Chapter 1: 2-6. The purpose in general is to give wisdom. And three classes of those to be helped are pointed out: the simple, the young, and wise men who may increase in learning. The purpose is not divorced from religion, but recognizes the necessity of religion: "The fear of the Lord is the beginning of knowledge" (1: 7, ASV). By seeking wisdom men shall "understand the fear of Jehovah, and find the knowledge of God" (2: 5, ASV). And again, "Jehovah giveth wisdom." That is to say *wisdom and religion* are *bound up together*: Seek wisdom in dealing with our fellow men and the common duties of life, and find God; seek God and find wisdom. For further illustration read Chapter 3: 13-26.

(3) This approach to life placed a constant emphasis upon the *true nature of wisdom.* Contrasted with folly, simplicity, and scorning, it "covers the practical and moral world as thoroughly as it does the intellectual" (Sampey). Wisdom is identified with righteousness and folly with wickedness (See 4: 11-14). Far from cutting men loose from the high demands and virtues of traditional morality, true wisdom binds men to purity and honor, to self-discipline and moral conquest.

(4) *The universal interest in life* is another mark of the Proverbs. There is, for instance, *no trace of*

racial bias or nationalism. The name of Israel is not mentioned in the entire book. "They were speaking to the heart on the common things of daily life that men of all races necessarily share with one another," says one. And Doctor Toy, in his commentary says, "If for the name Jehovah we substitute 'God' there is not a paragraph or a sentence which would not be as suitable for any other people as for Israel."

Also when we come to examine the many proverbs we find them touching *all sorts of men and all aspects of their lives.* The rich, the poor, the merchant, the housewife, sons, daughters, parents, fools and wise men, the lazy and the industrious, borrowers and lenders, the stingy and the generous, the boor and the flatterer, all find their portraits and a lesson. There is much criticism of conduct, but it *expresses no class prejudices.* After criticism comes positive teaching in proverbs that exalt the practical virtues which are commended to all. There are many counsels of restraint concerning appetite, anger and passion, and speech. Other proverbs commend industry, friendship, truthfulness, and kindness. The student of family life, or of social life will find much wholesome counsel.

Not all of these proverbs come up to the Christian ideal of individual character and social conduct. But *they have an upward reach.* They reveal in Israel a steady effort to improve life in all its details. They teach us that the little things of life are not unimportant, and that it takes discipline everywhere to make a perfect whole. And we are conscious as we read them that they are not out of place in a book of religion and revelation. As Doctor Elmslie (*Studies in Life from Jewish Proverbs*) expresses it, "They were not fortuitous atoms gathered no man knew whence or why, but part of a marvelous system inspired and originated of God, sustained by his inexhaustible power, and governed by his holy purposes."

2. *The Book of Job* manifests an approach to life similar to that of Proverbs. One difference is that

Proverbs is concerned with many problems and the problems of all sorts of people on things small and great. Job *deals with one great problem of a religious man*—the problem of suffering in a life consecrated and faithful to God. Another difference is that Proverbs answers the problems with sharp sword thrusts of "compressed experience," whereas Job answers in a great dramatic argument. Both conclude by exalting wisdom which begins in the fear of God and is found only in him.

(1) The Book of Job is a *dramatic poem.* It is based upon the experience of a man of Uz, whose story had come down from patriarchal times. This man suffered many afflictions, but stood them all, even though he had to stand them alone, without renouncing his faith in God. In a real way *Job's experience of suffering* paralleled the experiences of religious men in every age, and the book dealing with its problem might have been written in any century of Hebrew history. This is shown by the circumstance that scholars today place the *date of its composition* all the way from the time of Moses to the Exile; and none of them knows.

(2) *The plan of the book* is as follows: There is *first* a *prologue* in which Job is introduced as a righteous and prosperous servant of God. Satan, as Job's unknown adversary, obtains permission from God to afflict him, and so to test his faith, averring that under test he would renounce God. Then is given the story of Job's successive afflictions, which leave him in desolation, solitude, and unspeakable physical suffering. Three friends come and "mourn" silently with him (Chapters 1-2). The *second* part is a debate between Job and these three friends, in which the various theoretical explanations are affirmed by the friends on the basis of tradition, and denied by Job on the basis of experience (Chapters 3-31). In the *third* part a young man, Elihu, who has heard all, adds his idea, which differs from both Job's and that of the friends. (Chaps.

32-37.) The *fourth* part contains the sp
which does not explain Job's suffering, bu
to an overwhelming vision of the wisdom a
ness of God, before which he repents of
ings and bitterness (Chaps. 38:1-42:6). Th
with an *epilogue* in which God vindicates
stores his blessings and prosperity twofol

(3) The *interpretation of such a book* m
with great care and in view of the whole
not take a sentence out of the speeches o
friends, for instance, as truth, without "
with the rest of scriptural teaching. We
find light upon man's great adversary, up
acter of God, man's hope of immortality, an
ing of suffering. An excellent summary of
teaching is given by Doctor Sampey in *The*
Old Testament: "Afflictions may be sen
righteous as a trial of their faith. If pati
they lead to a higher knowledge of God, a
trust, a beautifying of character, and oth
They do not mean that God is angry with h
Moreover, God wishes his servants to trust
in the dark. He does not try to vindicate h
argument, but shows himself to the suffer
may widen and deepen his thought of God's
We can well afford to leave our case with th
ator and Preserver of all things."

3. *Ecclesiastes*, the third of the Wisdom B
still another light upon Old Testament life
deed "one of the strangest books in the Old T
and in its tone and temper one of the mos
It has in it a large number of proverbs, but
mixed in with a story of *a personal experien*
adventurous, disappointing, and perplexing
lem is not that of a pious man suffering aff
Job, but of an adventurous soul suffering d
ment.

(1) Notice first the *nature of a proverb.* Lord Russell described a proverb as "the wisdom of many and the wit of one." Another has said that it is *compressed experience:* "not one nor two but countless observations of men and things have gone to the making of a single proverb; it is the conclusion to which a thousand premises pointed the way; it is compressed experience." As such it is packed full of meaning. The writer just quoted advises on the basis of this fact that the proverbs yield greater results if we read few of them at a time and think long upon them. We cannot digest much of such strong food taken at once.

(2) What is *the purpose of the book?* Read Chapter 1: 2-6. The purpose in general is to give wisdom. And three classes of those to be helped are pointed out: the simple, the young, and wise men who may increase in learning. The purpose is not divorced from religion, but recognizes the necessity of religion: "The fear of the Lord is the beginning of knowledge" (1: 7, ASV). By seeking wisdom men shall "understand the fear of Jehovah, and find the knowledge of God" (2: 5, ASV). And again, "Jehovah giveth wisdom." That is to say *wisdom and religion* are *bound up together*: Seek wisdom in dealing with our fellow men and the common duties of life, and find God; seek God and find wisdom. For further illustration read Chapter 3: 13-26.

(3) This approach to life placed a constant emphasis upon the *true nature of wisdom.* Contrasted with folly, simplicity, and scorning, it "covers the practical and moral world as thoroughly as it does the intellectual" (Sampey). Wisdom is identified with righteousness and folly with wickedness (See 4: 11-14). Far from cutting men loose from the high demands and virtues of traditional morality, true wisdom binds men to purity and honor, to self-discipline and moral conquest.

(4) *The universal interest in life* is another mark of the Proverbs. There is, for instance, *no trace of*

racial bias or nationalism. The name of Israel is not mentioned in the entire book. "They were speaking to the heart on the common things of daily life that men of all races necessarily share with one another," says one. And Doctor Toy, in his commentary says, "If for the name Jehovah we substitute 'God' there is not a paragraph or a sentence which would not be as suitable for any other people as for Israel."

Also when we come to examine the many proverbs we find them touching *all sorts of men and all aspects of their lives.* The rich, the poor, the merchant, the housewife, sons, daughters, parents, fools and wise men, the lazy and the industrious, borrowers and lenders, the stingy and the generous, the boor and the flatterer, all find their portraits and a lesson. There is much criticism of conduct, but it *expresses no class prejudices.* After criticism comes positive teaching in proverbs that exalt the practical virtues which are commended to all. There are many counsels of restraint concerning appetite, anger and passion, and speech. Other proverbs commend industry, friendship, truthfulness, and kindness. The student of family life, or of social life will find much wholesome counsel.

Not all of these proverbs come up to the Christian ideal of individual character and social conduct. But *they have an upward reach.* They reveal in Israel a steady effort to improve life in all its details. They teach us that the little things of life are not unimportant, and that it takes discipline everywhere to make a perfect whole. And we are conscious as we read them that they are not out of place in a book of religion and revelation. As Doctor Elmslie (*Studies in Life from Jewish Proverbs*) expresses it, "They were not fortuitous atoms gathered no man knew whence or why, but part of a marvelous system inspired and originated of God, sustained by his inexhaustible power, and governed by his holy purposes."

2. *The Book of Job* manifests an approach to life similar to that of Proverbs. One difference is that

Proverbs is concerned with many problems and the problems of all sorts of people on things small and great. Job *deals with one great problem of a religious man*—the problem of suffering in a life consecrated and faithful to God. Another difference is that Proverbs answers the problems with sharp sword thrusts of "compressed experience," whereas Job answers in a great dramatic argument. Both conclude by exalting wisdom which begins in the fear of God and is found only in him.

(1) The Book of Job is a *dramatic poem.* It is based upon the experience of a man of Uz, whose story had come down from patriarchal times. This man suffered many afflictions, but stood them all, even though he had to stand them alone, without renouncing his faith in God. In a real way *Job's experience of suffering* paralleled the experiences of religious men in every age, and the book dealing with its problem might have been written in any century of Hebrew history. This is shown by the circumstance that scholars today place the *date of its composition* all the way from the time of Moses to the Exile; and none of them knows.

(2) *The plan of the book* is as follows: There is *first* a *prologue* in which Job is introduced as a righteous and prosperous servant of God. Satan, as Job's unknown adversary, obtains permission from God to afflict him, and so to test his faith, averring that under test he would renounce God. Then is given the story of Job's successive afflictions, which leave him in desolation, solitude, and unspeakable physical suffering. Three friends come and "mourn" silently with him (Chapters 1-2). The *second* part is a debate between Job and these three friends, in which the various theoretical explanations are affirmed by the friends on the basis of tradition, and denied by Job on the basis of experience (Chapters 3-31). In the *third* part a young man, Elihu, who has heard all, adds his idea, which differs from both Job's and that of the friends. (Chaps.

32-37.) The *fourth* part contains the speech of God, which does not explain Job's suffering, but brings him to an overwhelming vision of the wisdom and the greatness of God, before which he repents of his questionings and bitterness (Chaps. 38:1-42:6). The book closes with an *epilogue* in which God vindicates Job and restores his blessings and prosperity twofold (42: 7-17).

(3) The *interpretation of such a book* must be made with great care and in view of the whole. One could not take a sentence out of the speeches of Job or his friends, for instance, as truth, without "checking" it with the rest of scriptural teaching. We do, however, find light upon man's great adversary, upon the character of God, man's hope of immortality, and the meaning of suffering. An excellent summary of the central teaching is given by Doctor Sampey in *The Heart of the Old Testament*: "Afflictions may be sent upon the righteous as a trial of their faith. If patiently borne they lead to a higher knowledge of God, a deepening trust, a beautifying of character, and other rewards. They do not mean that God is angry with his servants. Moreover, God wishes his servants to trust him, even in the dark. He does not try to vindicate his ways by argument, but shows himself to the sufferer, that he may widen and deepen his thought of God's greatness. We can well afford to leave our case with the wise Creator and Preserver of all things."

3. *Ecclesiastes,* the third of the Wisdom Books, gives still another light upon Old Testament life. It is indeed "one of the strangest books in the Old Testament," and in its tone and temper one of the most modern. It has in it a large number of proverbs, but these are mixed in with a story of *a personal experience at once adventurous, disappointing, and perplexing.* Its problem is not that of a pious man suffering affliction, as Job, but of an adventurous soul suffering disappointment.

There is *much pessimism* in the story. The speaker is represented as Solomon—possessing every advantage of position, opportunity, and endowment. He starts out with high hopes of gaining happiness through learning (wisdom), but finds all is vanity and perplexity. He goes on in his pursuit by heaping up pleasures and luxury and great enterprises, but again is disappointed. His habitual question becomes, "What's the use?" In 2:24ff his thought turns to God as the giver of work and wisdom and knowledge and joy; but still he sees wickedness where righteousness ought to be, and when he lifts his eyes to the future he exclaims "Who knows?" and "What's the use?" So skepticism about God and the future, pessimism, and sometimes cynicism mark his speech. And the book shows how, when faith in God, hope of immortality, and loyalty to the high prophetic ideals, are lacking, the mere thinker and adventurer comes to despair.

But toward the close of the book the true wisdom of the wise men of Israel begins to appear. In 8: 12, ASV, he says: "Surely I know that it shall be well with them that fear God . . . but it shall not be well with the wicked . . .; because he feareth not God." And in 12: 13, ASV, as the "end of the matter," when all has been heard, he says: "Fear God and keep his commandments; for this is the whole duty of man." To this end of faith and loyalty toward God—the Creator and Redeemer and Eternal Hope of all men and every man, the whole Old Testament points. In its history, its prophecy, its worship, and its wisdom God is proclaimed as the answer to every human need.

REVIEW QUESTIONS

1. Why should we study the worship of the Hebrews? What guidance in this study do we have in the Bible?

2. What is meant by "wisdom"? What are the Wisdom Books?

3. What can be said about worship in the Bible before the days of Moses?

4. What revelation of the value of worship in the nation's life was made in the time of Moses?

5. Give a general description of the worship practices.

6. What was the attitude of the prophets toward worship and ceremony?

7. What do the Psalms indicate concerning the worship of the Hebrews?

8. Tell something of the history and authorship of the Psalms.

9. What is a proverb? What can you say concerning the origin and purpose of the Book of Proverbs?

10. What is the Book of Job? Give the plan of it.

11. What should be said about the interpretation of Job, and Wisdom Books in general?

12. How does Ecclesiastes differ from Job and Proverbs? Tell of its attitude, procedure, and conclusion.

FOR THE BLACKBOARD

The Book of Worship; of Wisdom

I. A Book of Worship
  1. The beginnings of worship
  2. Worship and the time of Moses
  3. The worship practices of the people
     Idolatry. Unreality
  4. The attitude of the prophets toward worship
     (1) Denounced false worship
     (2) Not opposed to ceremony
     (3) The personal nature of worship
  5. The Psalms
     (1) The national hymn book. Personal and national songs
     (2) The writing and collection of the Psalms
     (3) The Psalms as expressing the faith of Israel

II. A Book of "Wisdom"
  The meaning of "wisdom"
  1. Proverbs: practical wisdom about many things
     (1) The nature of a proverb

(2) The purpose of the book
(3) True wisdom as opposed to folly, and so forth
(4) A universal interest in life
Non-racial. Non-class. Upward reach in morals

2. The Book of Job: religious problems of a religious man
   (1) A dramatic poem. The problem. The date
   (2) The plan of the book
   (3) How to interpret such a book. The teaching

3. Ecclesiastes: problem of an adventurous soul suffering disappointment
   Compare Proverbs and Job
   Spirit and plan of the book
   The closing teaching

CHAPTER SIX

THE BOOK OF JESUS CHRIST

In the person and work of Jesus we come to the heart of the Bible. Both the Old and New Testaments get their life and meaning from him. In him the *history* of the Hebrew people finds its goal; *prophecy* finds its fulfilment; *worship* finds the unveiled presence of God; and *wisdom* finds its perfect light. He is the climax of progressive revelation and the perfection of religion. As Christian teachers, therefore, we must make him first in our study of the Bible. The disciples were not ready to preach until Jesus had opened the Scriptures unto them. Paul wholly misread the Law and the Prophets until he set Christ at the center of his thought and heart and life. And we, too, must know him, if we would understand the Scriptures and be prepared to teach them. One may be a Christian, knowing Christ in the personal experience of salvation, and have a very limited knowledge of the life and teachings of Christ. But one cannot be a worthy teacher unless he sets himself to know more and more about him in his person, his work, and his purpose. Howsoever much the Christian teacher may study the Scriptures and other sources of knowledge, he must begin and end with Christ, for he is the teacher's greatest teacher.

I. An Outline of His Story

We do not have a complete biography of Jesus. There are four books—Matthew, Mark, Luke, and John—which give selected portions of his story. The reason for the incompleteness is that each of the gospel writers wrote with a particular purpose in view. They were furnishing to the early church "evangelistic tracts" for use in witnessing. It has been noticed, for example, that *Matthew* wrote particularly for the Jews, and accordingly gave special attention to the life of Jesus as the fulfilment of Old Testament prophecy and to those words and works that had a more obvious reference to the Old Testament and to the life and ideals of the Jewish people. *Mark,* who wrote before the others, presents what he calls an "introduction" to the gospel, selecting materials that give a vivid picture of the busy ministry and the great power of Jesus as he moves on in his service to the world. The Gospel of *Luke,* the longest of the four Gospels, presents Jesus as the Saviour of both Jew and Gentile, enlarging upon his compassionate ministry to the poor and despised. Typical of Luke's emphasis is the word of Jesus, "The Son of man came to seek and to save that which was lost" (19: 10, ASV). The Gospel of *John* was written to show that Jesus was the incarnate Son of God. "It is the spiritual Gospel and was a bulwark against the Gnostics who denied either the real humanity of Jesus or his real divinity. The beloved disciple, full of spiritual insight and elevation, has given to the world his conception of the Christ which supplements the other Gospels and shows us the heart of Jesus." (A. T. Robertson.)

Combining the materials of these four books, we get the general sweep of Christ's life and work, if not the exact chronological sequence of all the incidents related. This general outline ought to be memorized by every teacher and the details filled in by continual study.

1. *From His Birth to His Baptism* (5 B.C. to 27 A.D.).

(1) Jesus was *born of the virgin Mary in Bethlehem* of Judea about 5 B.C., Joseph and Mary having gone thither from their home in Nazareth to be enrolled in the Roman census. Dr. David Smith calls it "the won-

drous birth," because, as the Scriptures tell us, it was not the beginning of a life, but an advent, "the Incarnation of One who had been from all eternity in the Bosom of God."

(2) *Four incidents of his early childhood* are related. First, *his circumcision* on the eighth day; second, his *presentation in the Temple* a month later, in accordance with the law (Lev. 12); third, the *visit of the Wise Men;* and fourth, the *flight into Egypt* to escape the hostile band of Herod who sought to slay him.

(3) Of *his boyhood* we have one glimpse in his visit to the Passover at Jerusalem, with Mary and Joseph, when he was twelve years old, the age at which he became a responsible "son of the Law."

(4) Of his *young manhood* we have only general knowledge. After their return from Egypt in Jesus' childhood the family settled at Nazareth. There Jesus grew up and was known as "the carpenter's son," and later as "the carpenter."

(5) *When he was about thirty years old* (about 27 A.D.) he left Nazareth and sought out John the Baptist, who was baptizing in the River Jordan. At his urgent request *John baptized him,* after which *the Holy Spirit descended upon him,* and the *voice out of heaven* said, "Thou art my beloved Son; in thee I am well *pleased*" (Mark 1: 11, ASV). Thus conscious of his Father's good pleasure he left his carpenter's shop behind and faced toward the mission for which he had come into the world.

2. *His Temptation and Early Ministry, Chiefly in Judea* (27 A.D.).

(1) Immediately after the baptism he was impelled by the Spirit to go into the Wilderness of Judea, which became for him the *wilderness of temptation.* There, as he fasted and meditated upon the mission that lay out before him, the *threefold temptation* came to him—

Pharisees who link him with Beelzebub and demand a sign; (b) the *increasing zeal of Jesus* and the concern of his mother and brothers for him; (c) the great group of *kingdom parables* recorded in Matthew 13, Mark 4, Luke 8; and (d) his *final visit and rejection at Nazareth.*

(3) *The third journey.* This also has its distinctive features. Matthew makes a point of the *extreme solicitude* of Jesus for the multitudes: "When he saw the multitudes, he was moved with compassion for them, because they were distressed and scattered, as sheep not having a shepherd" (9: 35-38, ASV). Also Jesus now *sends out the Twelve* before him to preach and heal, a fact which reflects the urgency of Christ and his desire to enlarge the experience of the disciples and train them to carry on.

4. *The Period of Withdrawals from Galilee* (six months; spring to fall 29 A.D.).

Within these six months the Gospels record four separate journeys outside of Galilee: (1) across the Lake of Galilee; (2) to the region of Tyre and Sidon; (3) to the region of Decapolis; and (4) across the Lake and on to the region of Cæsarea-Philippi. In explanation of these withdrawals two things must be remembered: first, his disciples' need of rest and of special instruction by him; and secondly the growing hostility of the religious leaders and of Herod Antipas, in conjunction with the excitement of the crowds who would have made him king.

(1) The *first withdrawal beyond the Lake of Galilee* was in order to find a place of quiet and rest for the disciples who had just returned from their first preaching tour. But they found no rest. The multitudes followed, and for Jesus it was a day of healing and teaching, climaxed by the *feeding of the five thousand* and the *efforts of the crowd to make him king.*

In Capernaum the next day he met some from the same multitude and gave the wonderful discourse on the Bread of Life which so sifted the so-called disciples that only the Twelve remained. He also was confronted by Scribes and Pharisees from Jerusalem who reproached him for disregarding the Jewish tradition.

(2) Soon, therefore, he was abroad again, this time toward the Northwest and the land of *Tyre and Sidon,* where he blessed the Syrophœnician woman.

(3) Without returning to Galilee he next went around the northern end of the Lake of Galilee and down on the east side to the region of *Decapolis* (ten cities), where he healed many and fed the four thousand.

(4) Again in Capernaum he encountered the Pharisees and Sadducees (traditional enemies now united against him) who persistently dogged his steps seeking to catch him and demanding a sign from heaven. Accordingly, he took his disciples away again across the lake and on toward the Northeast to the region of *Cæsarea-Philippi.* Here *three outstanding things occurred:* (a) Simon Peter made his *great confession,* "Thou art the Christ, the Son of the living God" (Matt. 16: 16, ASV); (b) Jesus told the disciples of *his forthcoming rejection, death, and resurrection;* and (c) Jesus was *transfigured* in the mount, talking with Moses and Elijah about his approaching death. From that time on his crucifixion and resurrection were often in his teaching, and he was speaking much with his disciples about the spirit of unselfishness and love with which they must serve in the kingdom.

5. *The Period of His Last Journeys* (six months: fall of 29 A.D. to spring of 30 A.D.).

After returning from Cæsarea-Philippi, Jesus did not remain long in Capernaum, but proceeded on down to Jerusalem to attend the Feast of Tabernacles.

(1) *In Jerusalem* as he *taught in the Temple* the *people were divided* concerning him and the *rulers*

sought to arrest him. In a great discourse recorded by John he *spoke of God as his Father* and *of himself as "the Son,"* and claimed to have been alive before Abraham. Whereupon the *people tried to stone him.*

(2) Until the Feast of Dedication (three months after Tabernacles) he remained *in Jerusalem and Judea.* His discourses were bold in their claims, in their denunciation of the Pharisees and lawyers for their hypocrisy, in his defense of himself, and in his demand for repentance if men would be saved.

(3) At the Feast of Dedication when the Jews tried to arrest him "he went forth out of their hand," and crossed over the Jordan *into Perea.* There he remained until summoned to Bethany by the sisters of Lazarus at the time of his sickness and death.

(4) From *Bethany,* where he raised Lazarus, he seems to have gone first *to Jerusalem,* thence *to Samaria and Galilee* and then to have started *southward again through Perea,* making his way for the last time *toward Jerusalem* for the final conflict. Many events and teachings and interesting persons are mentioned as of this fleeting period. One can hardly imagine the tenseness and the fulness of those last days when our Lord's face was set stedfastly toward the cross. After that brief and beautiful visit with Zaccheus *in Jericho* he journeyed on, and was soon in the beloved household *at Bethany* on Friday, one week before he was to be crucified.

6. *The Last Week and Crucifixion*

Because of the unfathomable meaning of the suffering and death of Jesus the story of this last week is given more space in the Gospels than any other part of his ministry. Here we give only the bare outline of his movements. On *Sunday* he made his triumphal entry into Jerusalem declaring thus his Messiahship and the peaceful nature of his kingdom. He returned to Bethany for the night. Again on *Monday* he was in Jerusalem where he cleansed the Temple of its unscrupulous and profane traders, and was greatly stirred by the desire of certain Greeks to see him. *Tuesday,* the last day of his public ministry, was one of the busiest days of his life. He was engaged in conflict with the rulers, Pharisees, Herodians, Sadducees, who confronted him with many snares and questions. Going out from the city in the afternoon he went first to the Mount of Olives with his disciples to whom he talked about the destruction of Jerusalem and his own second coming, giving the parables of the Ten Virgins and the Talents. When the day closed Jesus was back in Bethany receiving the beautiful anointing at the hands of Mary. The Jews were perfecting their plans to put him to death, and Judas was bargaining with them. As far as the records go *Wednesday* was a day of silence. On *Thursday* afternoon Jesus with his disciples went to the Upper Room in Jerusalem to observe the Passover together. After the institution of the Lord's Supper and wonderful words of assurance and comfort they went out to the Garden of Gethsemane. It was after midnight. There in the darkness he went through his great agony, and before day was betrayed into the hands of his enemies, who led him away. Early *Friday* he was rushed through the form of a trial, condemned, and led away to Golgotha. There they crucified him.

7. *His Resurrection, Appearances, and Ascension*

Buried in Joseph's tomb Friday afternoon Jesus' body was guarded by soldiers. But he could not be hindered by soldiers, nor holden by death. On *Sunday* morning he came forth from the tomb and showed himself to the women who had come to anoint his body. In the afternoon he appeared to his disciples also. For a period of *forty days* he appeared at intervals now to an individual and again to groups. His final appearance to his disciples was on the Mount of Olives, where he gave to them his *great commission*; and "while he blessed them, he was parted from them, and was carried up into heaven." In that brief ministry of forty days he "opened the Scriptures unto them," so that they saw both him and the Scriptures with new eyes. They saw him as the triumphant conqueror of death and the ever-living Saviour.

II. The Meaning of Christ for the World

The rest of the New Testament is a demonstration and interpretation of the meaning of the person and work of Jesus Christ for the world. To that the next two chapters will be devoted. But a summary is in order here, and perhaps no better view of our Lord's climacteric character can be given than that found in the great words used to identify and describe him.

1. *His personal name, Jesus,* is the Greek equivalent for the Hebrew "Joshua," which means "Jehovah is salvation." It was the name given through revelation by the angel to both Mary (Luke 1: 31, ASV) and Joseph (Matt. 1: 21, ASV) because it was he who should "save his people from their sins" and "reign over the house of Jacob forever." To the public it meant nothing more than the identification of the man, but to Joseph and Mary and to himself it had the deeper significance. When used alone in the New Testament it emphasized his humanity. He was Jesus, the man. Note, however, that it is usually connected with the word "Christ," either as "Jesus Christ" (Jesus, the man, who is the Messiah), or as "Christ Jesus" (the Messiah who is the man Jesus).

2. *He is also called Christ,* which is the Greek equivalent of the Hebrew "Messiah," the Old Testament word for the "anointed one" through whom God's promise to Israel would be fulfilled. To get the full significance of this term one must study the hope of Israel that runs throughout Hebrew history and the great Messianic prophecies.

The Old Testament is a book of hope. From the day of man's first sin there was a dream of recovery and victory over evil. In the heart of the race lived the hope of one day bruising the serpent's head (Gen. 3:15). It was the promise of God. When Abraham was called from Ur, it was made clear to him that God had chosen him to be a blessing to all mankind: "In thy seed shall all the families of the earth be blessed." See Genesis 12: 2-4; 13: 14-18; and especially 17: 1-8, ASV, where God made an everlasting covenant with Abraham, promising to raise up of his seed nations and kings and give them a land forever. This covenant was renewed to Isaac, to Jacob, to the Children of Israel in the time of Moses. As early as Moses' day this hope included the rise of a conqueror in Israel and of a prophet like Moses in the future. In David's day the promise was made to him that his seed should occupy the throne forever, and the figure of the great ideal king in his kingdom was celebrated in song. The Messiah of God would come and establish his everlasting kingdom in all the world (Psalms 2, 72, 110).

In the Period of the Prophets that hope was further brightened, especially in connection with the dangers that appeared in Assyria, Egypt, and Babylon. God would raise up a King, one whose name should be Wonderful Counselor, Mighty God, Everlasting Father, Prince of Peace, who would establish his kingdom forever. In him God would be present with the nation. Another prophetic picture was that of the Suffering Servant of Jehovah who will give his life to save the people (Isa. 53). So facing destruction Israel lived in hope,—one day God's promise would be fulfilled.

All was fulfilled in Christ. Not only in Matthew's gospel which emphasizes it, but in every part of the New Testament it is proclaimed. Jesus is the promised Messiah. In him the whole Old Testament is brought to focus and completion. He is the prophet like unto Moses, speaking with God face to face; he is the King, the Son of David, who will possess the kingdom forever; he is the Suffering Servant; he is the perfect High Priest who has made once for all complete atonement in his own blood (Hebrews). History, prophecy, worship, and wisdom are perfected in him.

3. *Jesus often called himself "the Son of man,"* a term used of the Messiah (Daniel 7:13f with Matt. 24: 30; 26:64), which also "gave expression to his sense of connection with all men in sympathy, fortunes, and destiny" (Stalker). His use of it emphasizes to us not only his humanity, but his identification of himself with all humanity, and his full consecration of himself to the salvation of the race (Mark 10: 45). He is our *Saviour.*

4. *The most glorious name of all is "Son of God."* He is God Incarnate. At the close of his earthly life which has been outlined so sketchily in this chapter he said to his disciples, "He that hath seen me hath seen the Father" (John 14: 9, ASV). The life of Jesus was the life of the Son of God, his words were the wisdom of God, his miracles were the power of God, his love and compassion were the grace of God, his cross was the suffering of God, his resurrection was the triumph of God over sin and death. This wonderful fact is on our lips when we call him *"Lord."*

Thus in Jesus, the Messiah, Son of man and Son of God, the various parts of the Old Testament and the New Testament are seen to be a movement of divine purpose leading on to the climax of redemption in God's Son. And the one comprehensive commentary upon the whole body of Scriptures in its organic unity is this: "God so loved the world that he gave his only begotten Son that whosoever believeth on him should not perish, but have eternal life" (John 3: 16, ASV).

REVIEW QUESTIONS

1. Describe the place of Jesus in history and revelation.

2. For what purpose were the Gospels written? Give the main characteristics of each of the four Gospels.

3. Give the general outline of the life of Jesus.

4. What are the principal recorded events in Christ's life from his birth to his baptism?

5. State briefly the meaning of Christ's threefold temptation.

6. Which Gospel tells of the early Judean ministry? What were the principal occurrences in that ministry?

7. How does Matthew (4: 23-25) describe the Great Ministry in Galilee? Name five or six of the outstanding facts or incidents connected with that ministry.

8. How do you explain the period of Christ's withdrawals from Galilee? What three great events took place at Cæsarea-Philippi?

9. Tell of the movements of Christ during the week in which he was crucified.

10. How long a time elapsed between the Resurrection and the Ascension? What are some of the great things that happened in that time?

11. Give the principal names applied to Jesus, and state briefly their significance.

12. Discuss more fully the significance of the name, Christ.

FOR THE BLACKBOARD

The Book of Jesus Christ

Jesus Christ the Heart of the Bible

I. An Outline of His Story
  1. From his birth to his baptism
    (1) Birth in Bethlehem. Outstanding facts
    (2) Four incidents of his early childhood
    (3) His boyhood
    (4) His young manhood
    (5) His baptism

2. His temptation and early ministry
   (1) The threefold temptation in the wilderness
   (2) The early ministry, for the most part in Judea
3. His ministry in Galilee
   Headquarters at Capernaum. Three journeys
   (1) First journey and after
   (2) Second journey and after. The Twelve
   (3) Third journey
4. The period of withdrawals from Galilee. Four journeys
   (1) The first withdrawal beyond the Lake. The 5,000
   (2) Withdrawal to borders of Tyre and Sidon. The Canaanitish woman
   (3) To Decapolis. The 4,000
   (4) To Cæsarea-Philippi. "Thou art the Christ"
5. The period of his last journeys
   (1) In Jerusalem
   (2) In Judea
   (3) In Perea
   (4) Through Samaria, Galilee, Perea, to Bethany
6. The last week and the Crucifixion
   Sunday, Monday, Tuesday, Wednesday, Thursday, Friday
7. The Resurrection, appearances and Ascension

II. The Meaning of Christ for the World
1. His personal name, Jesus
   His humanity. Deliverer
2. He is the Christ
   The Messiah of prophecy
   The hope of the Old Testament
   The fulfilment in Jesus
   Redeemer King
3. He called himself the Son of man. Meaning Saviour
4. He is the Son of God
   Incarnation—Lord

CHAPTER SEVEN

THE BOOK OF EARLY CHRISTIAN MISSIONS

We seek in this chapter an understanding view of the spirit, activities, and fruits of Christian men and women as they witnessed for Christ in that first century. There is a difference between learning an outline and seeing a movement that throbs with life. Apostolic history is a movement, the steady and progressive fulfilment of the promise made by Jesus on the day of his ascension: "Ye shall receive power, when the Holy Spirit is come upon you: and ye shall be my witnesses both in Jerusalem, and in all Judea and Samaria, and unto the uttermost part of the earth" (Acts 1: 8, ASV).

Much of the story of the early church is found in *the Book of Acts.* It was written by Luke, the physician and companion of Paul. He also wrote the Gospel which bears his name. As in the case of the Gospel his purpose in the Acts was not to write a complete history, but to give an orderly account of those events that marked the progress of the gospel in the progressive evangelization of the Roman Empire. It is noteworthy that he did not consider the expansion of Christianity as a new movement, but as a continuation of the ministry of Jesus through the Apostles and the churches by the power of the Holy Spirit. His Gospel was "concerning all that Jesus *began* both to do and to teach" (Acts 1: 1, ASV); the Acts recorded what he *continued* to do and to teach. The period covered extends from the Ascension of Jesus (30 A.D.) to Paul's Roman imprisonment (about 63 A.D.).

Although not historical in purpose the *remaining books* of the New Testament, especially the Epistles of Paul, contain historical material, and cast many side-lights upon the conditions of the time and the problems encountered both inside and outside of the churches. A complete view of New Testament history, therefore, must include a knowledge of all the books of the New Testament, for they were written in that period and reflect its life.

I. The Gospel of the Holy Spirit

Such is Dr. W. O. Carver's happy phrase for the Acts, to which others have given also the title "The Acts of the Holy Spirit." Both titles give proper emphasis to the fact that the sanctifying and moving power in the life of the early church was always and everywhere the Holy Spirit. One has only to read the book with this in mind to see their appropriateness. It is the Book of the Holy Spirit.

1. *The Coming of the Holy Spirit*

After the Ascension the disciples returned *to Jerusalem to the Upper Room* where they had kept the Passover with their Lord, and there waited, as he had commanded them to do, for "power from on high" (Luke 24:49). Besides the eleven Apostles certain women, Mary, the mother of Jesus, and his brothers are mentioned as being present. Luke says that in all there were "about a hundred and twenty" who resorted thither. There they prayed day after day. They *expected to carry on,* and were waiting for the promised power.

On the tenth day, *the Day of Pentecost,* "they were all together in one place. And suddenly there came from heaven a *sound* as of the rushing of a mighty wind, and it filled all the house where they were sitting. And there appeared unto them *tongues* parting asunder, like as of fire; and it sat upon each one of them. And they *were all filled with the Holy Spirit,* and began to speak with other tongues, as the Spirit gave them utterance" (Acts 2: 1-4, ASV). Three strange and significant things accompanied the gift of the Spirit: (1) the sound as of a rushing mighty wind—a symbol of the power which Christ had promised; (2) the tongues like as of fire—a symbol of speech by which they were to bear witness; (3) the ability to speak in foreign tongues—"a way of saying again, dramatically, that this Gospel of the Kingdom must be preached to every group in the language which the people best understand" (Carver).

The people of Jerusalem were greatly puzzled at what had happened, some thinking the disciples were drunk, but the disciples themselves understood. And Peter in a masterly sermon explained that God had poured out his Spirit upon them, and in the same sermon spoke with such power that 3,000 souls were converted. Thus the church entered upon its mission to the world in the power of the Spirit.

2. *The Abiding Presence of the Spirit*

(1) Among the witnesses *in Jerusalem.* From Pentecost onward the presence of the Spirit was observable. Glance along the pages of the Acts and see his work. "Filled with the Holy Spirit," Peter, who quaked with fear before the servant girl at the trial of Jesus, spoke boldly to the rulers (4: 8; 5: 32); and not only Peter, but all the others (4: 31). Stephen was unconquerable as he witnessed in the synagogue (6: 10), and, "being full of the Holy Spirit" was triumphant in his death. The Holy Spirit was also the secret of the shining life of Barnabas (4:36; 11:24).

(2) Among the witnesses *in Judea and Samaria.* When persecution arose and the believers were scattered abroad "in all Judea and Samaria" the Spirit was with them, encouraging their spirits, giving power to their witness. He was the guide of Philip in Samaria

and in his ministry to the Ethiopian (Chapter 8), and came in power upon those who believed through Philip's word. He commanded Peter to go with the messengers to the house of Cornelius (10:19), and came upon the household of Cornelius while Peter preached to them. In 9:31, ASV, Luke gives this summary of the witnessing in Palestine: "So the church (after the conversion of Saul) throughout all Judea and Galilee and Samaria had peace, being edified; and walking in the fear of the Lord and in the comfort of the Holy Spirit, was multiplied."

(3) Among the witnesses *in regions beyond*. It was the Holy Spirit who, while the disciples at Antioch were at worship, spoke and called upon them to set apart Barnabas and Saul (Paul) as missionaries to the Gentiles (13:2, 4). And the one explanation of the power of the missionaries in witnessing, and their courage under persecution, was that they were filled with the Holy Spirit (13:9; 52). When the difficulty arose concerning accepting the Gentile converts without circumcision the Holy Spirit guided in the decision (15:28). During the second of Paul's journeys it is said twice over that the Spirit hindered or forbade his going into certain regions (16:6, 7). And in 20:23 Paul speaks of a continual testimony of the Spirit to him concerning the sufferings that awaited him. In another place (20:28) he speaks of church officers as having been chosen by the Holy Spirit.

These references are given not to describe the whole work of the Spirit or the various forms of his manifestation. The point to be observed is that the Acts is indeed the Gospel of the Holy Spirit. The early church was Spirit-led in its witnessing, from Pentecost and Jerusalem on to Rome. We miss the meaning of the whole Christian movement if we miss that fact. And to leave that out of our teaching is to leave out the essential of Christian progress in any age—whether the sixth century or the twentieth.

II. The Witnesses

The early church grew by the personal witness of faithful men and women. And as in the case of the Old Testament the history of the New Testament hangs upon the framework of personal experience. It is the story of life spent in witnessing for Jesus Christ. Let us, therefore, seek to trace the Christian movement in a brief study of the Spirit-filled men who witnessed after Pentecost.

1. *The whole group, at Jerusalem under the leadership of the Apostles.*

It is a beautiful picture that Luke gives in Acts 2: 42-47, ASV. "All that believed" bore witness to the power of the gospel in their *fellowship and unselfishness.* They were together and "had all things common" in order that the need of every one might be supplied. They witnessed by their *worship and spiritual devotion.* They prayed, and sang hymns of praise; they ate the memorial supper together, and waited upon the teaching of the Apostles in the Upper Room and at other places as their numbers grew. They witnessed by their *spoken testimony,* and the Apostles were given power also to do "many *wonders and signs.*" The result was that they had "favor with all the people," and "the Lord added to them day by day those that were saved."

An example of the work of the Apostles during those days is given in *the experience of Peter and John* at the Beautiful Gate of the Temple. Turn to Acts 3 and note why the Apostles were there, what the experience was, and what were some of the results. The arrest of Peter and John on that occasion was the first persecution after Pentecost, in response to which the Apostles refused to stop their witnessing, and the whole group of disciples prayed to God for boldness with the result that their witness went forward with greater power (4:31), and their fellowship with one another was strengthened (4:32-37). The work of *Barnabas* is given special mention (5:36-37).

The witness of the Apostles under the leadership of Peter is further described in Acts 5. The *spirit of all the apostolic witnesses* is thus described by Luke after they had been beaten and charged to stop preaching: "They therefore departed from the presence of the council, rejoicing that they were counted worthy to suffer dishonor for the Name. And every day, in the Temple and at home, they ceased not to teach and to preach Jesus as the Christ." (Acts 5: 41f, ASV.)

2. *Stephen* occupies a special place among the early witnesses because he was *the first martyr.* He comes to our attention as a witness when the growth of the church and the problem of administration made it necessary to appoint seven men to take the relief work in charge (see 6: 1-6, ASV). Stephen was one of the seven, and is described as "a man full of faith and of the Holy Spirit," a man of "wisdom" and of "good report" in the church, and again as a man "full of grace and power" who "wrought great wonders and signs among the people." His zeal and power as a witness are seen in the circumstances that led to his death (6: 8ff). His great faith appears in the spirit in which he died (see 7: 54-60). Of great significance, also, is the fact that among those who heard Stephen's masterful and final testimony, and who witnessed his triumphant death was the young Saul of Tarsus, from whose soul the light of Stephen's countenance and the fire of Stephen's faith never departed.

3. *The Scattered Disciples.* Pushed to desperation by the growth of the Christian movement, the young Pharisee, Saul of Tarsus, raised the sword of persecution and compelled many believers to flee from Jerusalem to escape imprisonment. These scattered disciples became witnesses wherever they went in Judea, and Samaria (8: 4-40), Galilee (9: 31), Lydda and Joppa (9: 32ff), Cæsarea (8: 40; Ch. 10), Damascus (9: 2), Phœnicia, Cyprus, and Antioch (11: 19). Along the trail of these faithful men and women, fleeing for their

lives, was written a story of evangelism which adorns the pages of Scripture with the glory of the gospel, and gladdens the heart of humanity to this day.

Special attention is given to the witnessing of *Philip,* because he preached the gospel not to Jews only, but to the Samaritans (8:4ff) and to the Ethiopian (8:26ff), proclaiming to the Apostles and to the world that the gospel overleaps all racial and political and religious boundaries in its invitation and its power to save. Peter and John went from Jerusalem (where the Apostles had been permitted to stay) to see the strange procedure themselves, and as they returned they "preached the gospel to many villages of the Samaritans." The same expansion beyond the Jewish people was witnessed in Antioch where some of the fugitives, men of Cyprus and Cyrene, "spake unto the Greeks also, preaching the Lord Jesus" (11: 20, ASV). This result of persecution is not to be forgotten.

4. *Peter* is the only one of the Twelve to whom any great prominence is given in the Acts as a witness. This does not mean that the others were not busy and faithful (see 4:12; 6:2). John in the early stages was always at Peter's side (3:1ff; 8:14). The activity of James, John's brother, caused him to be put to death (12:2). But it was Peter's nature to be the spokesman, and so in a measure the witness of Peter may be taken as typical of the whole group.

We have already noted his leadership in Jerusalem in connection with Pentecost and subsequent events. When, however, the disciples were scattered abroad and the doors were opened to the Gentiles, the leadership had to pass to another. He preached to the Samaritans (8: 25) and to Cornelius (Chs. 10-11). He defended the preaching of the gospel to the Gentiles (15: 1-13), but was chosen for service among the Jews to whom he gave his greatest ministry. It is, therefore, because the Acts traces the expansion of the gospel among the Gentiles, and not because Peter stopped work, that we hear so little of him after chapter twelve.

5. *Paul* was the greatest among the New Testament witnesses. He is the same as Saul of Tarsus who scattered the disciples by persecution. He was destined as Paul the Apostle to scatter them throughout the Empire by his preaching. So abundant in labor was he, so gifted, so consecrated, so Spirit-filled that to trace his life is to trace the major line of Christian expansion after he entered upon his ministry.

(1) He was *converted* on the road to Damascus as he was going to that city on his mission of persecution. (see 9:1ff).

(2) *After his baptism* and a brief stay in Damascus he went away *into Arabia* (Gal. 1) where he remained in solitude—communing with God and getting his bearings, for something like three years. He returned thence *to Damascus* where he preached until the Jews were about to kill him (9:23-25). Escaping, he went down *to Jerusalem*, where he encountered much mistrust on the part of the disciples. He was, however, introduced favorably by Barnabas, and "preached boldly in the name of the Lord." Again the Jews sought to kill him, and he was sent by the brethren *to Tarsus*, where for some time he dropped out of sight (9: 26-30, ASV).

(3) *At Antioch* Paul really began his work as Apostle to the Gentiles. When the work among the Gentiles attracted the attention of the Apostles in Jerusalem they sent Barnabas to investigate (11: 22ff), with the result that he went over to Tarsus and brought Paul. For a year these two labored there together "and taught much people." Then came the call of the Holy Spirit for the beginning of the missionary career that occupied Paul the rest of his life (13: 1-3).

(4) *The three missionary journeys of Paul* and experiences growing out of them occupy the rest of the Book of Acts.

The first journey (13:13-14:28) upon which Barnabas and Mark were his companions, began with a brief ministry in the island of *Cyprus,* whence Barnabas had come (13:4-12). The main part of it, however, was *in Asia Minor* where amid hardship and persecution at the hands of the Jews many converts were made, and groups of disciples (churches) were left at *Antioch, Iconium, Lystra,* and *Derbe.*

Such an extensive and fruitful mission to the Gentiles inevitably raised the question whether Gentiles could be saved apart from circumcision or must accept the Law of Moses. Acts 15 tells of the *conference in Jerusalem* at which Paul and Barnabas, assisted by Peter and James (the brother of Jesus) convinced the leaders that the Gentiles ought not to be subjected to the Jewish ceremonial law. Christianity was not to be a sect of Judaism. It is to be noted, however, that Paul all his life had to contend with Jewish disciples who dissented from this position.

The second journey (15:40-18:22) led Paul and Silas, his companion, from Antioch, back again *into Asia Minor* to the churches that had already been established; and guided by the Spirit they came also into new territory as they came *to Troas* on the seacoast. Here occurred Paul's vision and call to cross over *into Europe,* and the four Christian missionaries (Timothy and Luke had joined the party) were soon across the Hellespont upon Christianity's greatest adventure. Successively they ministered for periods ranging from a few days to many months in the following cities, leaving in each of them vigorous groups of believers: *Philippi, Thessalonica, Berea,* and *Corinth.* Paul visited Athens also, but had no such success as in the other cities (17:16-34).

The third journey (18: 23-21: 15) took Paul from Antioch for the last time. It embraced much of the territory *in Asia Minor* that had been visited before, particularly *Galatia and Phrygia* where Paul's presence proved steadying and strengthening to the disciples. The one new field for Paul on this journey was *Ephesus,* where he remained for more than two years in a very rich ministry. The church at Colossæ and the seven churches of Asia Minor mentioned in the Book of Revelation no doubt shared in this movement whose center was at Ephesus.

After a visit to the churches of Macedonia (particularly Philippi) Paul made his way back, by way of Troas, Miletus, Tyre, and Cæsarea *to Jerusalem* where he was arrested at the instigation of the Jews.

(5) *Arrest and imprisonment* awaited Paul in Jerusalem. While he was in the Temple performing a vow he was set upon by the Jews. He was rescued by the Roman officials and later sent to Cæsarea for safekeeping until his case could be settled. After two years there, when it seemed that he was about to be allowed to fall into the hands of the Jews, Paul appealed to Cæsar and was accordingly sent *to Rome.* There he was allowed to live under guard in his own hired house, and was thus able to carry on his work, writing to the churches, witnessing to those who came to him, and counseling in the work of his helpers far and wide. The record in the Acts closes with the second year of the imprisonment. From other sources, especially his letters to Titus and Timothy, it is inferred with great probability that Paul came to trial and was released for a period of ministry in the East and perhaps in Spain; and that he was arrested in the Neronian persecution after the burning of Rome, and put to death about 68 A.D.

In these witnesses the promise of Christ had been progressively fulfilled. They had had persecution. Not a few had been put to death, or suffered exile, imprisonment and poverty. But the Holy Spirit had given them joy and courage and faith. The gospel had spread from Jerusalem, throughout Palestine and Syria, across Asia Minor, into Greece and in Rome itself a strong church lived. And according to Clement of Rome, Paul "had gone to the limit of the West," *i. e.,* to Spain even as he had purposed to do. All of this between 30 and 68 A.D.

III. The Churches

There remains for a brief glance one other factor in this New Testament history—the churches. The Lord Jesus Christ was the Head of the movement, and himself its gospel also; the Holy Spirit was its inward power and guide; the Apostles and other disciples were its witnesses and preachers and teachers; and the churches were its rallying centers, the homes of fellowship and unity, the conservators of faith and truth. The journeying witnesses did not leave new converts in isolation, but brought them together in little groups for fellowship, worship, instruction, mutual helpfulness, and for a common witness in extending the gospel yet further. Individual faith found, and must find, its best life, its strength and mission in association with like faith. Hence in the New Testament story we can trace the line of churches from Jerusalem to Rome—some of them strong, others weak; some centers of happy progress, others weighted with all sorts of problems and failures; all of them with human imperfections but drawn by the patient love of God.

1. *Jerusalem and Antioch.* These are mentioned together because they were respectively the centers of Jewish and Gentile Christianity.

Much has been said already about the glorious fellowship in Jerusalem in the months following Pentecost. (See Acts 1-7 again.) No more wonderful story of faith and power and courage can be written. It was when the gospel broke over the borders of the Jewish race, and the question of the essentials of the Christian religion as related to the Mosaic Law arose, that the Jerusalem church began to show its limitations. It questioned the preaching of the gospel to the Samaritans and sent Peter and John to investigate (8:14-16). It had Peter to justify his preaching and eating in the house of Cornelius, and baptizing his household without circumcision (11:1-18); and a skeptical attitude was very apparent. Again it sent Barnabas to Antioch in the same spirit (11:22). It was necessary for Paul and Barnabas to go to Jerusalem and have it out with the Apostles and brethren there concerning their Gentile mission (Chapter 15). To be sure, in every case they bowed to the manifest work of the Holy Spirit, but they would not lead. The environment of the Temple and ceremonial system, the Jewish traditions and prejudices were too much for them.

Accordingly, God gave the missionary leadership to the church at Antioch, and to Paul rather than to one of the Twelve. Henceforth Antioch was the center. Without prejudice it helped Jerusalem in its need (11:27-30). From it went forth the missionaries time and again with a gospel for all the world.

2. *The Churches in Asia Minor.* How many there were at the close of the Acts we do not know. From Paul's first journey we hear of *Antioch* (in Pisidia), *Iconium, Lystra,* and *Derbe.* From his other journeys and his epistles we learn much concerning the churches in *Galatia, Colossæ,* and *Ephesus.* And in the Book of Revelation there are brief letters to seven, including Ephesus, along with *Smyrna, Pergamum, Thyatira, Sardis, Philadelphia,* and *Laodicea.*

One must read the letters of Paul and the chapters in Revelation to get a picture of the life of these churches. They had to struggle and did struggle valiantly in a pagan environment for the preservation of their fellowship and faith and zeal for the gospel. Practical Christianity was as difficult then as now, and the Churches as churches faced problems like ours.

3. *The Churches in Europe* included those in the great centers of Philippi, Thessalonica, Corinth, and Rome,

to which Paul wrote. They were not all, for in many places little groups of Christians were joined together, but these represent the strength and progress of the Christian movement, and reveal the problems and difficulties which Christians had to face everywhere. *Philippi* comes as near to the ideal, perhaps, as any church of the New Testament. In writing to Corinth Paul holds Philippi (with other Macedonians) up as an example of liberality, and his Epistle to the Philippians reflects the beautiful life of the church. *Thessalonica* is typical of churches that go off at a tangent, taking hold of one doctrine, and that without true interpretation in their case, and giving it exclusive dominance. There the doctrine was the return of Christ. *Corinth* was the church of many internal difficulties—personal, moral, ecclesiastical and doctrinal, that created parties and wasted great gifts that ought to have made it a church of great spiritual and missionary power. *Rome,* at the meeting place of the highways of the world, was a strong, progressive, and influential church, so situated that it needed to be prepared with the completest understanding of the doctrines of Christ and the Christian life. It was to Rome therefore that Paul sent his greatest theological epistle.

These churches skirting the Mediterranean Sea on its eastern and northern sides, and a little later also on its southern coast (Alexandria), were the centers—"the pillars and ground of the truth"—from which the gospel would make its conquest of the Roman Empire and of the world. They were not perfect in their understanding, their character, or their activities, but they had the Spirit of life in them, and were used of God for his great redemptive purpose, as they struggled against their own inward imperfections and the dangers from without.

REVIEW QUESTIONS

1. What promise of Christ may serve as our outline of the early Christian missionary movement?

2. What book records the story of this movement? Who wrote it? And how did he think of the movement as related to Christ?

3. What is meant by "the Gospel of the Holy Spirit" as applied to the Acts? Tell of the circumstances preceding and at the time of the coming of the Holy Spirit.

4. Give an account of the work of the Holy Spirit among the witnesses in Jerusalem; also in connection with the missionary movement which began at Antioch.

5. Who are to be included among those early witnesses in Jerusalem? Who was the outstanding leader? Tell briefly of the witnessing of Stephen.

6. Why were the disciples scattered abroad? Name six places and regions they witnessed in.

7. Give in outline the ministry of Peter as recorded in the Acts. Why was his story not continued?

8. Give an outline of Paul's career.

9. What were the cause and outcome of the Conference in Jerusalem? (Acts 15.)

10. What were the most important things connected with Paul's second missionary journey?

11. Why did the church at Antioch become the center of the Christian movement?

12. Name the four principal churches established in Europe and characterize each briefly.

FOR THE BLACKBOARD

The Book of Early Christian Missions

Acts. The Writer. The Point of View. Other Sources

I. The Gospel of the Holy Spirit
  1. The coming of the Holy Spirit. The promise. Pentecost
  2. The abiding presence of the Spirit
    (1) Among the witnesses at Jerusalem

(2) Among the witnesses in Judea and Samaria
(3) Among the witnesses in the regions beyond

II. The Witnesses

1. The whole group at Jerusalem, under the leadership of the Apostles. Peter and John. Barnabas
2. Stephen
3. The scattered disciples. Philip
4. Peter
5. Paul, Apostle to the Gentiles
   (1) Conversion
   (2) After his baptism; Damascus-Arabia-Damascus-Jerusalem-Tarsus
   (3) Work in Antioch with Barnabas
   (4) The three missionary journeys
   (5) Arrest and imprisonment. Jerusalem, Cæsarea, Rome

III. The Churches

The places of the churches in the movement

1. Jerusalem and Antioch
2. The churches in Asia Minor. Most important names. General view
3. The churches in Europe
   Philippi. Thessalonica. Corinth. Rome

CHAPTER EIGHT

THE BOOK OF CHRISTIAN FAITH

It remains for us to look at the New Testament as the Book of Christian Doctrine, not with the purpose of discussing, or even mentioning all the teachings, but in order to see something of their sources and range, and how they came to expression.

One or two things should be kept in mind as we approach the New Testament in its doctrinal aspects. (1) Both Jesus and the Apostles had in their hands the Old Testament which was their Bible and the Bible of the Jewish world. Its high teachings about God, man, sin, divine mercy and redemption, its great ethical principles bearing on the personal and social moralities, were a part of their faith. This explains why many ideas of the New Testament are taken for granted and are not explained, much less defended. The New Testament stood upon the shoulders of the Old. (2) In the second place, neither Jesus nor any writer set out to give a complete and systematic statement of Christian beliefs. Paul in Romans is quite elaborate on some teachings, but even Romans is not a theology. The various doctrines came to expression in answer to the needs of the people and in particular situations. Hence we find varying points of emphasis as we pass from one writer or book to another. For instance, in Romans the emphasis is upon salvation by faith, in James upon good works, in Thessalonians upon the return of Christ, in Hebrews upon his high priesthood. Such facts as these ought to add interest and understanding in our approach to the doctrinal portions of the New Testament.

I. The Great Teacher

We must begin with Jesus, the Alpha and Omega of Christian truth, for all who came after him were only his interpreters. We have already made a survey of his wonderful ministry, tracing his movements and mercies to humanity as he made his way to his cross. Let us now be reminded that throughout the three years of his public ministry *he was constantly teaching.* Sometimes individuals (as Nicodemus, or the Samaritan woman, or the man whom he had healed), sometimes the multitudes by the lake or in the Temple, and again his chosen disciples in some quiet place, were his pupils.

He had *a passion for teaching.* "Take my yoke upon you," he cried, "and learn of me, for I am meek and lowly in heart: and ye shall find rest unto your souls." Truth burned within him for utterance, knowing as he did that by the truth he taught men might come into real knowledge and freedom (John 8: 31f).

Outstanding examples of his teaching are to be found in the *Sermon on the Mount* (Matt. 5-7) in which he taught the qualities of character that fit men for the kingdom of God, the meaning of righteousness, and the spirit of life in the kingdom; the *discourse on the Bread of Life* (John 6:22ff), in which he taught that he himself was the true bread sent from heaven, and that as men so receive him, and are sustained by him, they shall have eternal life; *the great parables,* scattered through his ministry, which he used to illustrate and explain to the discerning the truths of God's mercy and judgment, the meaning of brotherhood, the nature of the kingdom of God, and the rewards of sin and righteousness (See Matt. 13 for examples).

Jesus taught by his life and words, and by the miracles that he wrought. And the teacher may expect to be asked, *"What subjects did Jesus teach about?"* and, *"What did he teach about them?"* To be able to answer them there is a way much better than to depend on a book like this, and that is to *go to the Gospels themselves and follow through* the subjects we find upon his lips. For example, take the subject with which he began his ministry, *the Kingdom of Heaven.* What does he teach about it? Well, his very first utterance tells us something: that it is from heaven, that it is already at hand ready for people to enter it, and that men prepare for it by repenting of their sins. From that point we can track the word and the idea on through Matthew, finding much in the Sermon on the Mount, the great parables, and so forth. *The kingdom was one of the major subjects of his teaching.*

Another subject that was central in Christ's teaching was *the nature of God,* not so formally stated, but really that. He taught as no one else had ever taught that God is our *Father.* He always addressed God as Father and spoke of him as the Father. What did he say about the Father? Again go through the Gospels and find that the great attributes of God, such as his holiness, power, love, mercy, wrath, redemptive purpose, knowledge, are brought so close to life, and his presence so near, that we feel like pouring out our souls to the "Father who seeth in secret."

Other great subjects that run through the teaching of Jesus are *Himself* in his relation to the Father, and to men, and the redemptive purpose of his coming into the world and giving himself up to death; the *Holy Spirit; Eternal Life,* what it is and how it may be found; *Man,* with respect to his worth in the Father's sight, his need of salvation, and how he may be saved. And thus we might continue.

II. The Interpreters of Jesus

There are twenty-seven books in the New Testament. The writers of all of them get their inspiration, their subject, and their ideal from Jesus. They are his interpreters, seeking to make him known, and to bring into the world's life his truth and spirit and purpose.

It is well for us to know who they were and what they did as interpreters. Except in the case of the grouping of Matthew, Mark, and Luke, we shall take them in the general order of their writing.

1. *The Writers of the First Three Gospels.* Although the story recorded in these Gospels has been given, their writers ought again to be mentioned as interpreters of Jesus Christ. *Mark* selected certain materials and reported them in a certain manner peculiar to himself. He taught by emphasis that Jesus, our Lord and Saviour, was a man of action and full of divine power, worthy of worship in the world of powerful and imperial Romans. Over disease, sin, death, over animate and inanimate nature, over his own grave he has full authority. His *Lordship* is everywhere evident. Matthew interpreted him as one worthy of the faith and worship of all Jews in that he was the promised and long expected Messiah. The *Messiahship* of Jesus runs all through Matthew's record, while *Luke* interprets him in his compassionate ministry to high and low, rich and poor—to all the needy without respect of persons, as the Saviour of the lost. Luke is the Gospel of the *Saviourhood.* Together with *John,* who wrote to prove the *Deity* of Jesus, they not only recorded the materials which would be the foundation of the other New Testament interpretations of Christ, but gave their own separate and composite doctrines.

2. *James,* the brother of Jesus and leader in the Jerusalem church, in his epistle deals with Christian attitudes and conduct which are the natural fruit of faith. His book reminds one of the Sermon on the Mount. Some years ago Dr. A. T. Robertson wrote a book on James whose title, *Practical and Social Aspects of Christianity,* exactly describes its contribution to Christian doctrine. It is the doctrine of practical righteousness as the moral demand and fruit of Christian faith.

3. *Paul,* the greatest of missionaries, was also *chief among the interpreters of Jesus.* Thoroughly taught in the Old Testament as a young Pharisee, after his conversion he gave himself, mind and soul, to know Christ. He was familiar also with the churches of Asia Minor and Europe, and with the problems and heresies that arose to hinder and confuse them. Accordingly, with their burden always upon his heart, he gave himself not only *in a tireless journeying* that he might teach and preach in person, but *in a series of letters* on matters pertaining to Christian faith and life. Our perspective of his teaching through these letters (thirteen in number) will be helped by noting that they group themselves around *certain leading subjects* as follows: (a) Christ's second coming; (b) the relation of Christianity to Judaism; (c) questions concerning the Person of Christ; and (d) practical matters of a personal and pastoral nature. It should be noted also that the letters to the churches are usually divided into two distinct parts, *doctrinal and practical,* or faith and morals.

(1) *The second coming of Christ is the leading subject of 1 and 2 Thessalonians.* (52-53 A.D.) Misinterpreting what Paul had said on the subject when he was there, some of the Thessalonians had been blinded to the mission of the church and the ordinary duties of life. Paul wrote, not to take their eyes off the future, but to make their faith in the second coming and the great inheritance a source of strength, comfort, and inspiration.

(2) *The relation between Christianity and Judaism* became a question as soon as Gentiles began to accept Christ. Must Gentiles be circumcised in order to be saved? Were they under obligation to observe the Mosaic Laws? Was Christianity an independent religion or a sect of Judaism? Many Jewish Christians insisted on Judaism as the basic faith. Paul insisted that Christ is the all-sufficient Saviour, and that men are saved by faith in him and not by circumcision or by the

works of the Law. How widespread that controversy was is indicated by the letters in which Paul dealt with it: *1 and 2 Corinthians* (in Greece); *Galatians* (in Asia Minor); and *Romans* (in *Italy*).

(a) In *the letters to Corinth* (about 57 A.D.) many other subjects are dealt with, but prominent and running throughout is the all-sufficiency of Christ apart from the Law. See especially 1 Cor. 8-9 and 2 Cor. 3.

(b) *The letter to the Galatians* (about 57 A.D.) is called by Dr. A. T. Robertson "a bugle blast for freedom from Jewish ceremonialism." At the very heart of the letter Paul says, "Before faith came, we were kept in ward under the law, shut up unto the faith which should afterwards be revealed. So that *the law is become our tutor to bring us unto Christ,* that we might be justified by faith" (3: 23f, ASV).

(c) *The Roman letter* (probably 58 A.D.) is in many respects the greatest of all the epistles. Its great subject is *the righteousness of God,* which is the need of all men, Jew and Gentile alike, and which comes to all alike by faith. Read 3:21-30 for a burning answer to the Judaizers. In chapters 5 to 11 is an elaborate discussion of the blessed *results of faith in Christ,* in which he shows that the fruits of faith are far beyond what men found in the observance of external laws. It means reconciliation and peace with God; it means death to sin and life unto God; it means partnership with the Spirit in prayer and in bearing all our infirmities; it means victory and eternal fellowship in "the love of God which is in Christ Jesus." In Romans and his other epistles in his teaching about Jesus, Paul develops as an essential element in Christ's sufficiency the doctrine of the Cross, the sacrifice of Jesus for the redemption of men. "He died for us" is at the heart of Paul's gospel.

(3) *The Person and place of Christ* became a subject of grave concern in Paul's latter days as he saw the rise of heresy concerning him, particularly in the region of Colossæ in Asia Minor. Although that heresy

seems not to have been outspoken in Philippi and Ephesus, it was in his mind as he wrote to the churches in those centers, and so he took occasion to emphasize the exalted character and redemptive work of Christ. His teaching concerning Christ marks the high point in the prison epistles, *Philippians, Ephesians and Colossians.* See especially Philippians 2: 5-11 in which he gives his view of Christ in his deity, humiliation, death, exaltation, and final triumph; and also the first two chapters of Ephesians.

In Colossians Paul came to direct grips with the Gnostics who denied both the deity and humanity of Jesus, making him a sort of emanation from God who mediated between God and man. To that Paul answered in that wonderful passage (1: 15-18, ASV), saying that Christ is "*the image of the invisible God,* the first born of all creation; for *in him were all things created,* in the heavens and upon the earth, things visible and things invisible, whether thrones or dominions or principalities or powers; all things have been created through him and unto him; and he is *before all things,* and *in him all things consist.* And he is *the head of the body, the church:* . . . that in all things he might have the *preeminence.*"

Besides the strictly theological subjects Paul's teaching included many others touching church life, the Christian ministry and service in the church, personal morality, social ethics, and so forth. One group of epistles deals particularly with matters personal and pastoral (*1 and 2 Timothy and Titus*). *Philemon* shows how Christian love operates and should operate in a difficult social situation such as slavery. And all the epistles already mentioned have their great sections of practical Christian instruction. See Romans 12ff. The Corinthian letters also are treasuries of Christian ethical and social interpretations.

4. *Peter* is credited with two general epistles which were probably written in Paul's last year (65-67 A.D.). He was not the theologian that Paul was, but a true

teacher of the truth he heard from the lips of Jesus, nevertheless. What he taught in his speech, if not elaborated in his epistles, is suggested in three wonderful verses of his first letter (1: 3-5, ASV), "Blessed be the God and Father of our Lord Jesus Christ, who according to his great mercy begat us again unto a living hope by the resurrection of Jesus Christ from the dead, unto an inheritance incorruptible, and undefiled, and that fadeth not away, reserved in heaven for you, who by the power of God are guarded through faith unto a salvation ready to be revealed in the last time." How many Christian doctrines are mentioned in that one sentence! In the letters he teaches the blessedness of life under God's grace, and the Christian hope in the second coming of Christ, and gives various counsels for moral and social behavior, exhorting to stedfastness in the truth, and courage in the midst of persecutions.

5. *Jude,* a brother of Jesus, in a brief letter probably to the Christians of Syria and Asia Minor, seeks to steady their faith against heresy and immorality, by reminding them of the truths taught by the Apostles, mentioning briefly some of the doctrines. The burden of his letter is in verse 3, ASV: "Contend earnestly for the faith which was once for all delivered unto the saints."

6. *The Author of the Epistle to the Hebrews,* whose name we do not know, wrote for Jewish Christians who were being tempted by persecution and otherwise, to abandon Christianity for the old Jewish faith. The point of Paul's argument in Galatians and Romans was that Gentiles are free from the Mosaic Law, that Christianity is not a reformed Judaism, but itself the way of salvation. The point of Hebrews is that *Christianity is superior to Judaism,* being God's revelation of himself through his own Son. The whole claim centers in the Person, Office and Work of Jesus Christ the Son of God, the perfect High Priest, and Saviour.

Dr. A. T. Robertson's outline of the Epistle in his *Student's Chronological New Testament* presents the doctrine and purpose of the book so clearly that we give it here: Christianity is superior to Judaism because (1) Christianity came not through prophets, but through the Son of God (1:1-3); (2) Christianity came not through angels, but through the Son of God (1:4-2:18); (3) Christianity was not given through Moses and Joshua, but through Jesus (3:1-4:13); (4) Christianity has a better priesthood than that of Judaism since Jesus is (a) a better High Priest than Aaron (4:14-7:28), (b) the minister of a better covenant (8:7-13), (c) minister in a better sanctuary (9:1-12), (d) offers a better sacrifice (9:13-9:18), and (e) works on the basis of better promises (10:19-12:3). There follows inevitably in the rest of the book a great exhortation to stedfastness to Christ, the Apostle and High Priest of our confession.

7. *John,* the beloved disciple, was a faithful teacher and witness through many years, being the last of the Twelve to die (around 100 A.D.). He wrote *the fourth Gospel* in order that, as he says, "ye may believe that Jesus is the Christ, the Son of God; and that believing ye may have life in his name" (20: 31, ASV). We have also from his pen *three epistles,* the last two being very brief and personal.

The first epistle expresses more at length the concern revealed in the others. John makes an argument for holy living. Christianity is a religion of goodness. Sin is corruption, and separates from God. We need forgiveness and cleansing for which the blood of Christ alone is sufficient. The supreme motive of the Christian life is love for God and one another. And love is of God, for God is love. The great manifestation of that fact is Jesus Christ, whom God sent to be the propitiation for our sins, to be our Saviour. After fifty years John is teaching what he and Peter taught back in 30 A.D.,—that there is no other name: "He that hath the Son hath the life; he that hath not the Son of God hath not the life (1 Jno. 5: 12, ASV).

The last writing of John, and the last in the Bible, is the *Book of Revelation* (about 95 A.D.). Written from his island prison in the midst of persecution and gloomy prospect, it is Christianity's answer to conflict and suffering. It teaches the final triumph of Christ over his enemies, the overthrow of Satan, and the consummation of the kingdom of God. Its imagery is difficult, but its teaching is clear if we do not permit ourselves to be lost in the maze of details. Its vision of the throne, its songs of salvation, and its faith in the triumphant return of Christ strengthened the churches in difficult days.

III. The Teachings Classified

As a conclusion of this chapter it is desirable that we get a perspective of the teachings of the New Testament. How may they be classified? And how would one answer inquiries concerning the range of New Testament doctrine and the great subjects that are central? Let us suggest a threefold classification, which we trust may be of service to the advancing teacher as he, with Bible in hand, seeks to fulfil his ministry of teaching.

1. *The Theological Teachings.*

In times past this class of teachings received almost exclusive interest in Bible school work. When one said doctrine one meant theological doctrine, matters of faith. We have passed from that, and in some quarters there is a growing aversion to teaching the basic theological doctrines. The need is for equilibrium, remembering that these doctrines are the foundation upon which the other teachings are based, and in which men find the true highway of life which alone leads to their highest destiny. Of greatest importance, therefore, are such leading doctrinal subjects as the following:

(1) *Concerning God.* Here upon the background of Old Testament revelation we follow Jesus and the other teachers as they speak of God *as Father* with his moral holiness, perfect and eternal love, over-watching providence, and redemptive purpose. We then see him *incarnate in his Son,* who is one with the Father, as in power and wisdom and love he works out through compassion, humiliation, and sacrificial suffering, man's salvation from sin and death. We find him also in *the Holy Spirit,* who is God present in his Spirit, called also the Spirit of Jesus, directing his Church, dwelling in his people to instruct, strengthen, guide, and sanctify them. Wonderful things are written concerning the nature and activities of this Divine Trinity.

(2) *Concerning man,*—his worth in God's estimation, his lost condition, his possibilities in respect to character, service, and destiny in Christ.

(3) *Concerning sin* in its nature, its fruits of corruption in the race, its condemnation, and as God's problem in his purpose of redemption.

(4) *Concerning salvation* as man's need and God's desire for him, as the work of God through the life, death, and resurrection of his Son, as the gift of his grace through faith which he kindles in the hearts of men.

(5) *Concerning the Church*—the body of Christ to do his will in the world.

(6) *Concerning the Kingdom of God* in its spiritual, moral, and social nature, in the principles and methods of its growth, and as the consummation for which men are to labor and pray.

2. *The Ethical Teachings.*

In all the Epistles there are sections on the Christian life. And much the greater portion of the reported teachings of Jesus is moral, rather than theological. Moral teaching grew out of the basic doctrines, but it grew. Christianity neglects the study and teaching of Christian ethics at its peril. Sincere and well-intentioned believers have done much damage in society and brought reproach on our religion, because they were ignorant of the moral and social teachings of the New Testament. Learn and teach what the Scriptures say:

(1) *Concerning the qualities of Christian character.* From the Beatitudes to the end of the New Testament traits of goodness are taught as God's demand. It was the lack of *reality* that brought condemnation upon the Pharisees. Beginning at that foundation stone of reality or sincerity the stature of a full-grown man must be built up.

(2) *Concerning the principles of social conduct.* Life must be lived among men, and there is a Christian way, and a pagan way, of living it. What are the principles which should direct a Christian in his home life? In the church? In his neighborhood? In his business? As a citizen? Here there is also a basic principle, *love,* which is the unifying and conserving bond about all the social virtues. The New Testament has guidance for us; we lack moral understanding because having eyes we see not, and having ears we hear not.

3. *The Missionary Teaching.*

Christian people are in the world on a mission. From beginning to end the Bible is a missionary book. The New Testament is the product of the missionary spirit, and is full of missionary passion and instruction. *Faith* and *life* are to be developed and sanctified in *witnessing.*

(1) Concerning *the principles and motives of missions* Christ and Paul and the others speak in terms of divine authority and call, human need, Christian love, and the essential Christian spirit.

(2) Concerning *the horizon of missions,* we hear the words of Jesus, "the whole creation," "all the world," "beginning at Jerusalem," "unto the uttermost part."

(3) Concerning *the agency of missions,* the New Testament speaks of individuals and churches responding to the Holy Spirit.

(4) Concerning *the end of missions,* it speaks a word of hope and triumph. In its picture we see "a new humanity," the kingdom of God come, the will of God done on earth as in heaven. These appear in the purpose of Christ and in the prayer which he planted in the hearts of his missionaries.

REVIEW QUESTIONS

1. What two things should be kept in mind as we approach the New Testament as a book of Christian teachings?

2. Discuss Christ's teaching ministry and spirit, with some examples of how he taught.

3. Give the subject and central idea of some of Christ's principal teachings.

4. What is the central teaching of each of the four Gospels concerning Jesus?

5. Write briefly of James and Jude and their epistles.

6. What central subjects and controversies called forth the Epistles of Paul?

7. In what epistles did Paul discuss the relation between Christianity and Judaism? What in brief did he teach?

8. What other subjects does Paul discuss in 1 and 2 Corinthians, and Romans?

9. In what epistles did Paul discuss particularly the doctrine concerning Christ? What occasioned the discussion? Give the outstanding points in the teaching.

10. Give the purpose and teaching of the Epistle to the Hebrews.

11. In what books did John give his interpretation of Christ and the Christian faith? What are the purpose and meaning of the Revelation?

12. Give a classification (without discussion) of the New Testament teachings.

FOR THE BLACKBOARD

The Book of Christian Faith

Two Things to Be Kept in Mind

I. The Great Teacher

Jesus constantly teaching. His passion for teaching. Outstanding examples of his teaching. His great themes

II. The Interpreters of Jesus

1. The writers of the first three Gospels
   Mark: The Lordship of Jesus
   Matthew: The Messiahship of Jesus
   Luke: The Saviourhood of Jesus
   John: The Deity of Jesus
2. James, the brother of Jesus
   The practical and social aspects of Christianity
3. Paul. Thirteen letters. Leading subjects
   (1) The second coming of Christ, discussed in 1 and 2 Thessalonians
   (2) The relation between Christianity and Judaism, in letters to the Corinthians, Galatians, Romans
   (3) The person and place of Jesus Christ, emphasized in Philippians, Colossians, Ephesians
   (4) Matters pastoral and personal occupy large place in letters to Timothy, Titus and Philemon
4. Peter. Two general epistles
5. Jude, brother of Jesus. A brief epistle against heresy and immorality
6. The author of the Epistle to the Hebrews. Jesus the High Priest and Saviour. Robertson's outline
7. John, the apostle. The fourth Gospel; three epistles, Revelation

III. The Teachings Classified

1. The theological teachings
   (1) Concerning God
   (2) Concerning man
   (3) Concerning sin

(4) Concerning salvation
(5) Concerning the church
(6) Concerning the kingdom of God

2. The ethical teachings
(1) Concerning the qualities of Christian character
(2) Concerning the principles of social conduct

3. The missionary teachings
(1) Concerning the principles and motives of missions
(2) Concerning the horizon of missions
(3) Concerning the agency of missions
(4) Concerning the end of missions

CHAPTER NINE

THE TEACHER AND HIS BIBLE

The Sunday school is a Bible school. The Bible is the Sunday school teacher's fundamental textbook. It is the starting point, the foundation of all that the Sunday school seeks to contribute to the life of mankind. Its simple stories, its challenging precepts, its profoundest doctrines, all find a place in the scheme of instruction. And that because *the church is conscious of its teaching mission and the world's need of what the Bible contains.* Those who are lost need its message of redeeming grace. Those who are saved need its light and power. Without its guidance even the well-intentioned soul is unable to find and keep the true highway. Without its power the journeying Christian must meet the enemy in an unequal conflict.

In Bunyan's *Pilgrim's Progress* it was when "the Sword of the Spirit, which is the Word of God," flew out of Christian's hand that Apollyon had the courage to exclaim, "I am sure of thee now"; and it was only when Christian had caught up that Sword again that he was able to give the strong enemy a deadly thrust. In our day many Christians are letting the Sword fall from their hands. *The Bible is for many homes and hearts a lost book, and the Sunday school teachers are God's chosen men and women to re-discover and recover it* for the boys and girls, young men and women, fathers and mothers of our generation. It is a great task. How shall the teacher go about it? How can he prepare to make good in the thing he is attempting? What importance shall be attached to preparation, in the light of what he is trying to do? Where shall he look for encouragement?

I. Light from the Great Teacher

We turn first to Jesus. *He is the world's greatest teacher.* Measured by the highest standards of the first century or the twentieth, he merits the crown of excellence and perfection. In character, in spirit, in the truth he taught, in equipment, in method, in ideals, and in the fruit of his teaching in the life of the world, he is the central Sun about whom lesser lights circle with varied glory. We must turn to him first when we seek the best in teachers and teaching. Accordingly as we inquire concerning the teacher's esteem and use of his Bible we open our New Testament with this question in mind: *"What place did Jesus' Bible (the Old Testament) occupy in his heart and mind?"* And we make a rich discovery.

1. *He knew his Bible.*

(1) When he encountered the temptations in the wilderness, the sword with which he beat back Satan was his Bible, quotations from the Book of Deuteronomy: "Man shall not live by bread alone, but by every word that proceedeth out of the mouth of God"; "Thou shalt not tempt the Lord thy God"; and "Thou shalt worship the Lord thy God and him only shalt thou serve."

(2) When he appeared before his fellow townsmen in the synagogue at Nazareth to announce his mission he "opened the book and found the place" in Isaiah 61, which set forth the things he had been anointed of God to do.

(3) The Sermon on the Mount besides its direct quotations is full of references or allusions to Old Testament history, law and prophecy, establishing the fact of most extensive knowledge and clearest insight.

(4) Throughout his ministry as he met inquiring souls and faced his enemies he used many direct quotations and made numberless allusions to biblical records. He quoted from memory words from Genesis,

Exodus, Leviticus, Deuteronomy, Samuel, Hosea, Isaiah, Jeremiah, Daniel, Zechariah, Malachi, and Psalms 8, 22, 110, 118. So thoroughly did he know the Sacred Writings that his vocabulary was stamped with their distinct imprint.

(5) When he was dying on the cross his anguish found expression in the words of a Davidic psalm: "My God, my God, why hast thou forsaken me?"

(6) And after his resurrection he took his disciples apart and "opened to them" the Scriptures, carrying them through the Sacred Books, and opening their minds to what was said there concerning himself.

2. *He learned his Bible by diligent study.*

Believing in the true humanity of Jesus, we must believe that *he learned his Bible as other men learned it.* He was reared in a Jewish home in which religion was at the center, which meant that as a boy he was taught, like Timothy, by his mother. At the age of twelve his heart drew him to the teachers in Jerusalem, where he listened and asked questions, as well as answered them. He no doubt attended the synagogue school as other Jewish boys did. *He grew* in wisdom; *he advanced* in wisdom, that is, literally, he "cut forward," implying his initiative and diligence, the use of his faculties of thought, imagination, memory, applying his wonderful spiritual nature and passion to the possession of all that his Father had spoken to Israel.

Jesus learned his Bible. *It fed his soul.* Its psalms became his songs; its prophecies his strength and encouragement. In its words he heard the Father's voice. And as the promise and foundation of his mission he took its words into his heart, that he might pass them on to others, stripped of the barnacles of human precepts and prejudices, and shining with the lustre of his own divine words of grace and truth. Surely even as he, so ought every servant of his, called to teach, be an untiring student of the Bible. If we would be teachers we must first be students. Paul was not speaking of an option, but of a necessity when he wrote to Timothy: "Give diligence (study) to present thyself approved unto God, a workman that needeth not to be ashamed, handling aright the word of truth" (2 Tim. 2: 15, ASV).

II. The Teacher as Bible Student

1. *The Sunday school teacher's aim,* therefore, in this matter of preparation must be a *progressive knowledge of the Scriptures.* This is *a work of patience and persistence,* for the Bible is a great library. Volumes have been written on every one of the sixty-six books, and on many of them great libraries. It is not a bad sign, therefore, when a teacher says that he "knows so little about the Bible"; the bad sign is up when he stops trying to know more. Knowledge is a progressive thing, and everybody starts with a minimum. It is all *a matter of progress and the price in diligence and persistence that men are willing to pay.*

Very important also is *the kind of knowledge* the teacher should seek. The Pharisees in Jesus' day had a very extensive knowledge of the Scriptures, but theirs was *a mere literal knowledge* without common-sense understanding. They could quote it; they knew the letter of it, but not the spirit, ignorant of the fact that "the letter killeth, but the spirit giveth life" (2 Cor. 3: 6, ASV). The Sadducees knew a great deal about the Bible also, but theirs was *a critical knowledge.* They went to it with certain preconceptions and prejudices. Certain things they rejected on "rational" grounds before they ever considered the testimony of the Scriptures. They read with closed minds, seeing only what they wanted to see, or to raise questions concerning things they did not believe. To them, when they came with one of their questions, Jesus said, "Ye do err, not knowing the scriptures, nor the power of God" (Matt. 22: 29, ASV). When we speak of knowing the Bible we do not mean, then, memorizing it or knowing all the difficult questions that may be asked about it. They have their place, but it is secondary. *True knowledge is understanding.* For examples of the difference between the knowledge of the Pharisees and Sadducees and that of Jesus turn to Matthew 5: 21-48 and 22: 23-33. True knowledge sees principles as well as words, positive and practical values for conduct as well as doctrinal problems for the intellect. True knowledge majors on principle and practice; spurious knowledge on precept and problem. The teacher ought to know these latter, but he ought not to leave unknown the weightier matters of principle and practice.

2. *With what spirit and attitude should the teacher approach the Bible?* In view of the error of the Pharisees and Sadducees the first thing to be said here is that the teacher's *Bible study must not be primarily professional, but personal.* Referring to Paul's three references to the gospel as "the," "my," and "our," Dr. J. D. Jones once said, "*The* gospel must become *my* gospel before it can become *our* gospel." By his own study the teacher should seek to have those experiences of spiritual and cultural enlargement in his own life, which he seeks by his teaching to produce in the lives of his pupils. This means personal and practical study. "Received merely into the mind, and regarded as a subject for discussion or debate, the truths of the Scripture do not nourish the soul. It is when we lay aside the weight of controversy and approach them as a hungry man does his meat, that we gain their satisfaction" (Cadman).

To become the best kind of teacher, one must not only study for his own development, but *in a spirit of reverence and devotion.* One should remember what the Bible is, whence it came, for what purpose it was given, what blessings of grace it contains. Something of this attitude is expressed in the words of the great theologian and teacher, Dr. William Newton Clark, on the subject, *Why I Love the Bible*: "Because it glows with the light and love of Christ; because it showed me Him who walked the earth and hung upon the cross that He might save such men as I; because it brings me what He revealed of the living God and Father whom to know is life eternal."

"Because it shames me, inspires me, and calls me upward. It is the Book of faith and hope and love, of comfort, holiness, and power, of salvation and eternal life. It is my truest visible guide to the right knowledge and experience of God, the true estimating of myself and my life, and the spirit in which I may live worthily with men."

"Because out of it I may gather, and have gathered, a little book most precious, a Bible from within the Bible, which I bind to my heart and carry in my memory and live with in light and darkness, a treasure of the strongest and sweetest words of the soul that were ever known."

3. *The teacher must not despise discipline and method in his study.* His must be a *planned* study, and he must establish the habit of *constant* study. Being a very busy person during the week the Sunday school teacher may not be able to give long periods of time to the Bible, but they can be made frequent and regular.

In preparing *for the individual lesson* there are at hand the lesson helps in quarterlies, teachers' manuals, and general works such as commentaries and dictionaries, which are suggested in the literature of the Sunday School Board from quarter to quarter. *For his wider and general knowledge of the Scriptures* the Board is furnishing in its Training Course for Sunday School Workers at least five other books in direct Bible study. Given in training schools and for private study, all these books ought to be mastered by those who undertake to teach.

In addition to these prescribed preparations there are *many methods* by which one may achieve a constantly progressive understanding of the Scriptures.

All cannot be followed at once, but by changing from one to another one may avoid monotony and preserve a lively interest.

(1) The first to be mentioned is that which should accompany and be a part of every other, namely, *daily Bible reading,* in which one gets not only the "run" of the Scriptures book by book, but, if it is done unhurriedly and prayerfully, those daily thoughts and inspirations which give a glow to living.

(2) Another method is *by books.* For example, take the Gospel of Matthew upon which were based the Uniform Lessons for six months in 1934. Not all of it, of course, could be covered by the lessons, but the teacher had a wonderful opportunity of studying the whole book. There are to be had at small cost excellent guides to such study, which give outlines, introductory information about the author, the writing of the book, the historical, religious, and social backgrounds, and the interpretation of the book. By the use of these one can come into a definite acquaintance with the gospel, and get a clear view of Matthew's portrait of Jesus. More often than not the Sunday school lessons follow a book of the Bible for at least a quarter, and so furnish an incentive for this sort of study.

(3) Closely related to this is the study *by periods.* Refer, for example, to the outline of Old Testament History. In any given period one has before him the historical facts, the activity of the prophets, with such of their books as were written in the period, the religious conditions as reflected in the worship, moral conditions, and so forth.

(4) The study of *the great characters* of the Old and New Testament is rich in its rewards. To take them in chronological order would give a very comprehensive view of the external history of the Bible, as well as a new appreciation of the leading personalities in that history. To become thoroughly acquainted with the life, character, and writings of Moses, or

Jeremiah, or Paul, is worth much more than a dim and unimpressive knowledge of all of them.

(5) One may also find great reward in a knowledge of the ideas and doctrines of the Scriptures in *tracing the use of great words.* Doctor Jowett, the noted English preacher, took great delight in this kind of study; it ought to be just as delightful to a Sunday school teacher. Think, for example, of "running down" such words as repent and repentance; faith, faithful, faithfulness; forgive and forgiveness; light, darkness; sin, transgression, rebellion; love, and hundreds of others. To follow these through, noting the speaker, the circumstances, the purpose, the probable meaning, and so forth, is a game at once entertaining and blessed.

III. The Teacher as Bible Interpreter

The teacher is an interpreter. James felt the gravity of this fact when he wrote, "My brothers, do not swell the ranks of teachers; remember, we teachers will be judged with special strictness" (James 3:1, Moffatt). *What is an interpreter for?* In his *Pilgrim's Progress,* Bunyan has two very suggestive passages. In the first, Christian is arriving at the house of the Interpreter, who asks him what he would have; and Christian makes this reply: *"I am a man that am come from the City of Destruction and am going to the Mount Zion;* and I was told by the Man that stands by the Gate at the head of this way, that if I called here *you would shew me excellent things, such as would be a help to me in my journey."* That is the work of an interpreter. The second passage is a song found on the lips of Christian as he left the Interpreter's house to pursue his journey alone:

"Here have I seen things rare and profitable;
Things pleasant, dreadful, things to make me stable
In what I have begun to take in hand;
Then let me think on them, and understand
Wherefore they shewed me was, and let me be
Thankful, O good Interpreter, to thee."

Such is the fruit of the interpreter's work well done. Doubly emphasized, therefore, is all that has been said about Bible study, by the fact that the teacher studies for himself and another. By what methods the teacher should seek to interpret the Scriptures is a subject which belongs to another. Here we desire to suggest, however, the meaning and the end of Bible interpretation.

1. *What do we mean by interpretation?* Stated briefly it is taking an idea of one person and presenting it to another in such a way that he gets an accurate understanding of it. That it is a difficult undertaking can readily be seen. Take as an example a recent Sunday school lesson on Christ's parable of the Ten Virgins. In order to give a true interpretation of that parable the teacher must know (1) what it says. If he lazily or ignorantly misstates the language he must go wrong from the start. (2) He must know how to interpret parables. There are certain principles to be applied as, for instance, that he should look for one principal truth in a parable. Usually also Christ's parables are not allegories, in which every detail has a symbolical meaning, but stories in which details are largely just the shell in which the kernel of truth is couched. The teacher must apply these principles, asking what kind of parable it is, and what the central message is. (3) He must ask, "What did Jesus mean?" Often in our zeal to bring lessons we give slight attention to, or miss altogether, the idea the writer had in mind. *The interpreter must do everything possible to get into his own mind exactly the ideas that Jesus had in mind.*

Even then the difficulties are not all behind him. *He must get the idea unchanged into the mind of his pupil.* How difficult this is every experienced teacher knows. Explain something very carefully next Sunday morning and then make a test of the fulness and accuracy with which you got your idea across. One soon learns that *the pupil plays about as great a part in interpretation as the teacher.* He is not a jug to be poured full through a funnel. He is a personality who must not only accept what he receives, but reach out and get it, if it is to mean very much to him in a crisis. And so the difficult task of the interpreter is so to present the idea, or the story that contains it, or the character that exemplifies it, that the student will reach out to know it. How that is to be done the book on teaching will suggest. The point here is that there are three parties in interpretation—the truth, the teacher, and the pupil, and the work of interpretation is not easy, either in getting or in making known the idea.

2. What now, let us ask in conclusion, is *the end of the interpreter's work?* Two things assuredly stand out:

(1) *To glorify the Heavenly Father* by making his truth known. We have said that the Bible is the Word of God. In it is the supreme revelation of himself in Jesus Christ. In it we find the gospel of divine redemption, the way of salvation. As the teacher gives himself to learning and teaching the Bible he is helping to bring in the glorious day when the knowledge of God will cover the earth as the waters cover the sea.

(2) *To open the minds of the pupils* to what God has spoken, so that they will have *a new interest* in the Scriptures, a *new and growing faith* in God, and *a new will to press on* toward fuller knowledge of the Word of life. To the true teacher the Bible is more than a library of sacred literature; it is more than a multitude of facts, historical, theological, and ethical, to be learned; it is more than a textbook to be taught; it is God's message of redemption and life. To teach it to growing souls is a commission in whose fulfilment no cost is too great to be paid.

REVIEW QUESTIONS

1. Why must the church continue to put greatest emphasis upon the Bible as the Sunday school textbook?

2. What place does Jesus occupy among teachers? What place did the Bible occupy with him?

3. Give several scriptural witnesses to Christ's knowledge of his Bible.

4. How did he come into this knowledge? Quote 2 Tim. 2: 15.

5. What should be the teacher's aim as a student of the Bible? What kind of knowledge of the Bible should he seek? Compare the kinds which the Pharisees and Sadducees had.

6. With what spirit and attitude should the teacher approach the Bible?

7. What help is offered the teacher in his study by the Sunday School Board?

8. What are some recommended methods of Bible study?

9. What is meant by saying that the teacher is an interpreter?

10. Discuss the difficulty of interpretation.

11. What twofold end does the Christian interpreter seek?

12. To you as a teacher, what is the Bible?

FOR THE BLACKBOARD

The Teacher and His Bible

I. Light from the Great Teacher
   1. He knew his Bible. Illustrations [(1) to (7)]
   2. He learned his Bible

II. The Teacher a Bible Student
   1. The teacher's aim—a progressive knowledge of the Scriptures
      Different kinds of knowledge
   2. The spirit and attitude of the teacher
      Personal *versus* professional. Reverence and devotion
   3. Necessity of discipline and method
      Accessible materials. Various methods
      (1) Daily Bible reading

(2) By books
(3) By historical periods
(4) By following great characters
(5) By tracing great words

III. The Teacher as Bible Interpreter

What an interpreter is for

1. The meaning of interpretation. Example. Three questions
2. The objective of the interpreter
   (1) To glorify the Heavenly Father
   (2) To open minds and hearts to understand and accept the truth of God